F

ALSO BY KEVIN NELSON

Baseball's Greatest Quotes
Baseball's Greatest Insults
The Greatest Stories Ever Told (About Baseball)
Football's Greatest Insults
The Greatest Golf Shot Ever Made

Baseball's Even Greater Insults

KEVIN NELSON

A FIRESIDE BOOK • PUBLISHED BY SIMON & SCHUSTER
New York London Toronto Sydney Tokyo Singapore

F

FIRESIDE
Simon & Schuster Building
Rockefeller Center
1230 Avenue of the Americas
New York, New York 10020

DESIGNED BY BARBARA MARKS
Manufactured in the United States of America

1   3   5   7   9   10   8   6   4   2

Library of Congress Cataloging in
Publication Data

Nelson, Kevin, date.
Baseball's even greater insults/Kevin Nelson.
p.   cm.
"A Fireside book."
Includes index.
1. Baseball—United States—Miscellanea.
2. Baseball—United States—Quotations,
maxims, etc.   3. Baseball—United States—
History.   I. Title.
GV863.A1N44   1993   92-32597
CIP

ISBN 0-671-76066-1

Contents

Now
They Tell Me...

"Don't say 'Greatest.' Nobody believes it anymore. I think there are more 'Greatest's' than Baseball's'. Any day now, somebody will write 'The Greatest Mundane Commonplaces.' "
—Author Bob Carroll, giving advice to would-be authors on what to title a baseball book.

In 1984, with the publication of *Baseball's Greatest Insults*, a new age dawned in America's national pastime. For the first time ever baseball fans could turn to one definitive, absolutely essential text to find out all the dirty rotten things that players, managers, umpires, owners and the media ever said about one another. The game has never been the same since.

Okay, so I exaggerate a little.

But *Baseball's Greatest Insults* did indeed come out, and I am very glad it did. And now we have *Baseball's Even Greater Insults*, covering the past decade. In the last 10 years or so much has happened in baseball of an insulting nature. The Wade Boggs adultery scandal, the Steve Garvey paternity scandal, the Pete Rose gambling scandal, the Luis Polonia she-was-fifteen-going-on-twenty-nine scandal, the George Steinbrenner–Howie Spira payola scandal, the Al Campanis "Am I an idiot or what?" scandal, the Rob Dibble wild man with a fastball scandals, the Roger Clemens "Read My Lips" scandal, numerous Jose Canseco driving scandals, and illegal substance scandals galore. For guys in my line of work, this has been a terrific decade for baseball.

For those who may have missed the original *Baseball's Greatest*

Insults and are not familiar with the concept, I should explain that you will find nothing here about "the poetry" of the game or the timelessness and universality of baseball and how what the game is really all about is fathers playing catch with their sons. There will be no lyrical passages extolling the great green balllyard and what a magical, mystical oasis it is. Nobody from the *New Yorker* will be quoted in this volume; nobody from the *New Yorker* would probably even *read* a book of this type. Nor will there be any passages in this book from a certain pompous windbag bowtie-wearing, right-wing, stuffed-shirt Cubs fan, although we do insult him whenever possible.

In this book you will get guys like George Brett describing one of his teammates, "He looks like a greyhound, but runs like a bus," or Tom Paciorek talking about A's manager Tony LaRussa, "Tony couldn't manage a fruit stand." Or Frank Luksa, a sportswriter, remarking that "Mitch Williams has walked more people than a seeing eye dog," or Tony Kornheiser joking that the oft-injured reliever Don Robinson "hopes to become the first reliever wheelbarrowed in from the bullpen." That kind of thing.

So go ahead. Dig in, and enjoy. And as a final note, let me say thanks to Mark Chester and George T. Kruse, two fine photographers who came through when I needed them.

—KEVIN NELSON

A Short History of Baseball (Part II)

On August 7, 1991, Schottzie, the 160-pound St. Bernard who was the mascot of the Cincinnati Reds and the close companion of Reds owner Marge Schott, was put to sleep after being diagnosed for terminal cancer. Laid to rest in a Reds baseball cap, Schottzie was buried in a private ceremony in the rose garden of her master's home. She was nine.

The day after her death, during a game at Riverfront Stadium, Roger McDowell, a reliever for the Los Angeles Dodgers, wore a black armband with a white paw print in memory of Schottzie.

"It's like losing a part of the baseball family," said McDowell. "Babe Ruth died. Lou Gehrig died. Now Schottzie."

And Now, A Look At The Game Today

Brett, Reggie, Murray, Kingman—now, wait a second, that was the *last* book. This is *Baseball's Even Greater Insults*, the long-awaited sequel to *Baseball's Greatest Insults*. You'll have to excuse me, it's going to take a while to get up to speed here. This is the nineties, and now we're talking names like Jose, Darryl, Kirby, Cecil, Roger, Wade, Margo, Barry, Bret, Fay (Fay?), Cal, Will, Eric, Rob, Dwight, Ryne and . . . *George?* Egad, is he still around? Yes, unfortunately, he still is, but you won't have to hear about him until much later.

For now let's turn our attention to a man who, despite being the greatest base stealer of all time, remains one of the most modest and unassuming superstars in the game today, an ebullient Ernie Banks–type character who just loves to play no matter what they pay him. You know of course who we're referring to . . .

The Incredibly Beloved Rickey Henderson

According to a 1987 survey of major league ballplayers conducted by the publishing conglomerate of Nash-Zullo, Inc., Rickey finished first in the following categories:

- "Players Who Always Complain About Their Aches and Pains"
- "Which Players Complain the Most to Plate Umpires"
- "Players Who Make Easy Catches Look Hard"
- "Players Opposing Teams Love To Hate"

Hamming it up for the press, Rickey Henderson lays a smacker on his 100th stolen base in 1982, the year he went on to set the all-time single season stolen base mark.

And Rickey took third—behind Mel Hall and No. 1 Dave Parker —in still another category: "Who Are The Biggest Showboats After Hitting Home Runs?"

In conclusion, then, Rickey's ballplaying peers consider him to be a chronic whiner and complainer who showboats unmercifully and is widely disliked. As the columnist Glenn Dickey puts it, "When it comes to dogging it, nobody is in a class with Rickey Henderson. The A's outfielder may not be the highest-paid player, but he is certainly the highest paid canine." Woof, woof!

Great Moments in Rickey Henderson's Career

Greatest Moment: May 1, 1991, Oakland, California. Rickey steals No. 939, breaking Lou Brock's career stolen-base mark. They stop the game for the award ceremony and, with Brock standing beside him, Rickey utters the immortal words, "Lou Brock was a great base stealer, but today I am the greatest of all time." Padres reliever Larry Anderson says later that Rickey's comments "made me want to puke." Columnist Sean Horgan adds, "Perhaps the problem with our ozone layer is that Rickey's ego keeps punching holes in it."

Second Greatest Moment: In 1989 Rickey signs a $3-million-a-year contract, making him the highest paid player in baseball. Over the next year salaries explode (again), dropping Rickey from the top of the ladder to well down in the league. Rickey demands to renegotiate. The A's say no, and suggest compromise proposals that Rickey won't accept. So Rickey goes into a sulk. "What, you want me to play like Mike Gallego?" he says, insulting a teammate. Then he stages a spring training holdout. Then he lays down like a dog for the 1991 season.

What does Rickey really want? *Inside Sports* magazine offers a theory: "More. Rickey wants more. Rickey demands more. Whatever he makes on his next contract, Rickey is asking for more. The minute he agrees to any new deal, Rickey intends to insist on more. 'You can never get enough more,' says Rickey. 'I deserve more. I expect more. I am more.' "

Or, as Carleton Fisk says, summing up the feelings of baseball fans everywhere: "How can a guy making $3 million be underpaid? They [players who complain about being underpaid] can go kiss my ass."

A Little Note about Carleton

Now Carleton Fisk can put the hammer to the greed-ravaged ravings of Rickey Henderson, but let's not forget that back before Fisk's age and remarkable durability elevated him to the status of Baseball Icon, a great many people did not care for *his* personality, either. Frank Robinson thought he was a snot. "He's the most disliked player in the league because of the way he struts that walk and the way he won't give in to anyone," said Frank.

When Carleton came up to the majors in the early 1970s, a cocky young New Englander on New England's team, he walked that walk and he talked that talk. And it irritated the hell out of some of his peers. After the Red Sox traded Reggie Smith, another man of no small ego, to St. Louis in 1973, Carleton publicly agreed with the move. "The loss of Reggie's bat will be outweighed by the loss of anxiety and disrupture that Reggie occasioned," he said haughtily.

Smith in turn called Fisk "a backstabber and a crybaby" and carried his anger over to the following year when the Cardinals and Red Sox met in spring training, the first time the two men had seen each other since the trade. During the game a pitch bounced up and caught Fisk square in the balls and as the future Hall of Fame catcher writhed on the ground in pain, Smith, watching from the dugout, yelled out, "I hope you die, motherfucker!"

Darryl

For the most part, connoisseurs of The Insult do not hold much truck with born-again Christians. Not that we have anything against them or their new-found beliefs. It's just that, well, how many down-and-dirty insults has Scott Garrelts ever said? Or Brett Butler? Or Orel Hershiser? Orel goes on Johnny Carson and sings a hymn, for Christ's sake. Very sweet, very poignant, but not exactly what we had in mind for *this* volume.

Darryl Strawberry, however, has proven the exception to the born-again blandness rule. He's shown that you can embrace God and still fire off some ill-humored, ill-tempered remarks at your fellow man. For instance, after the Mets awarded Bret Saberhagen his old number (18) for the 1992 season, Darryl didn't like it one bit: "After all the good years me and the Mets had together, all the winning, they give my number away just one year after I'm gone. It's an insult to me. It makes you wonder what the people in the front office are thinking."

One of his teammates on those old Mets was Gregg Jefferies, who left New York in the Saberhagen trade. Strawberry has criticized him as well. "Seems to me he can't handle the pressure," Darryl told sportswriter Bob Klapisch. "Look at who they got rid of because of Jefferies. Wally [Backman], Tim Teufel, even Howard Johnson had to play short, and [Kevin] Elster had to sit down because Jefferies had to be at third. Those guys might not have had the same talent, but I've never seen them pull themselves out of a game."

The Straw continued, "They thought he could carry them when I left, but Jefferies is too worried about his hitting, always crying about some slump he's in. Tell him the only way he's going to make it . . . is if he concentrates on his whole game. No more taking his 0 for 4 onto the field. I've seen it too many times, even now." And finally, when asked if he had any sympathy for Jefferies, Darryl did not exactly resemble St. Francis: "Sympathy? I have no sympathy for him at all. Jefferies hasn't had nearly the pressure I had."

When Darryl played for the Mets he was, in Brett Butler's words, one of those "immoral slobs who lives his life in the pits of hell." Since then he has joined the Dodgers, gotten religion, and apparently purged himself of his slobness. But in 1991, his first season with LA, even his fellow born-agains on the Dodgers were wondering about him. Butler said he looked listless. Gary Carter said he seemed to lack the fierceness he had in New York. One writer called him "as inspirational as a statue." Dodgers manager Tommy Lasorda was more to the point: "This guy hit 37 home runs last year. Did he forget how to hit?" But Darryl's bat came back to life in the second half of the season and so did his mouth.

In late May, after being whiffed by Houston's Al Osuna, Strawberry told reporters, "He doesn't have anything I can't handle." Osuna's dad, who lives in the Los Angeles area, saw the quote in the paper and relayed it to Al, who swore never to forget. The next time the rookie reliever faced Strawberry he struck him out again and then issued this challenge: "Every time I face him, he's going to get everything I have. If he ever gets a hit off me again, I'll be upset. Every time he comes up there, I'll be looking to strike him out." Darryl did not turn the other cheek. "He's a rookie talking a lot of smack," he said. "I'll see him down the line, and we'll see what he can do. I don't want to get into it with guys like him. He hasn't been around long enough to talk smack." Darryl did indeed see Osuna down the line. In September they faced each other a third time, and the

Straw hit a three-run home run off him in the bottom of the 10th to win a game.

Despite such heroics the Dodgers finished a disappointing second that year—a result that the once-passive Strawberry blamed on his teammates' passivity. "This was a team where after a good play, half the guys would shake your hand and the other half . . . I don't know what they'd be doing," he said.

In the off-season Darryl got more specific, attacking fellow outfielder Kal Daniels as "a cancer" on the team and saying he should be traded. "I don't want to deal with what we dealt with last year, a guy like Kal, a player who doesn't want to play. Trade Kal. If he doesn't want to play, get him out of here. And you can quote me on that." Strawberry hammered away, "Somebody has to finally say something about him, and I'll be the guy. I'm talking about us needing somebody who is determined to play with injuries, somebody who won't get kicked out of a game in the first inning in the pennant race, somebody who always wants to be there."

Daniels, a friend of Strawberry, was shocked: "I love the guy like a brother, but if he is going to back-stab me like that, evidently he has a mental problem. If he back-stabs me like that and we're supposed to be friends, what does he do to players he doesn't like?" Kal didn't much like Strawberry's attitude: "Darryl signed the big contract and he thinks he's all-world. Well, he's not. The first half of the season he was invisible. If he doesn't want to play with me, well, the feeling is mutual."

Ironically, the things Strawberry said about Daniels are much like what Strawberry's former teammates on the Mets used to say about *him* —that he faked being sick, complained constantly, and couldn't be counted on in a pinch. But that's a story for another chapter ("Ballclubs From Hell," the 1987 New York Mets). Seeing that it's probably better to take Darryl in small doses—even a born-again Darryl—we'll move on.

Taunts
Or, Some Fans Offer Constructive Criticism of Their Ballplaying Superheroes

"Hey, Snack Bar! Get that hamburger out of your pocket!"
—Insults yelled at the rotund Tony Gwynn

"Hey, Jose, how's Madonna. Where's Esther?"

—A New York fan, heckling Canseco about his love life and marital woes; (Canseco, who also had an inflatable Madonna-lookalike doll thrown at him in New York, reportedly had to be restrained from punching the guy).

"Hey Joey, keg party at my house after a game. Wanna come?"

—One of the barbs directed at Indians outfielder and recovering alcoholic Albert (formerly Joey) Belle, who hit the fan who said it with a baseball in a notorious 1991 incident

"Where's Lenny? He out drinking?"

—A San Francisco fan, waving a set of car keys and yelling at a Phillies player after teammate Lenny Dykstra's near fatal drunken driving accident.

"Kirk Gibson! Kirk Gibson!"

—A favorite taunt of fans whenever Dennis Eckersley pitches.

What Players and Others Think about Fans and Their Use of Their First Amendment Rights at the Ballpark

"A bunch of dirt-mouthed, uncivilized, uneducated people."
—Eric Show, pitcher

"Albert should have hit the guy in the head."
—Pitcher Norm Charlton, after Belle hit that fan in the chest with a baseball after being taunted for his alcoholism

"Not many men up there would allow the type of things that were being said about their wife and mother. Those things are unacceptable. A guy [who] pays his way into the stadium is allowed to hoot, but there is a line."
—A's manager Tony LaRussa, after fans heckled Jose Canseco at a wild and woolly Yankee Stadium game

"Fans have gotten out of hand. They are getting away with things that, if they did them on the street, would be called assault. It isn't good for the games, the players, the fans."
—Stan Kasten, Atlanta Braves executive

"The more I think about it, the clearer it is that it's the fans who are pushing the limits of good taste. Heaping torrents of sick, angry, ugly abuse on players—who do they think they are? Jack Clark?"
—Scott Ostler, columnist

Jack Clark, Journeyman Slugger, Sounds Off

On American League umpires: "Now I know why Billy Martin threw dirt on them. He tried to cover them up and make them disappear."

More on American League umps, comparing them to their brethren in the National League: "They're awful, they don't have a clue. I don't know if they don't practice or what. They've got a lot more lowlifes there."

On playing for Frank Robinson in San Francisco in the early eighties. "He resented me making $1.3 million, supposedly because of the caliber of player I was compared to what he was. He did everything in his power to make it uncomfortable for me, constantly comparing me in the paper: I'm not as good as this guy or that guy, comparing me to guys even on our team. How's that supposed to make me feel?"

After Robinson played him when his knee was injured: "You want to try to hurt me for the rest of my life? Fuck you. Go die. I'll never play for you again."

On playing for the 1982 San Francisco Giants: "This organization is a loser."

In the final days of the 1987 pennant race, Clark's Cardinals couldn't take batting practice until the football Cardinals (then mainly "replacement" players substituting for the striking regulars) finished working out at Busch Stadium. Said Jack: "That's the worst I've ever seen. Here we're trying to win a pennant. We've got four days left and the fucking scabs are on the field taking up our time. Unbelievable. If they're there [again] I'm going to hit line drives at their butts and see if they catch them. They ought to send those scabs back to Yugoslavia or wherever they came from."

On former Cardinal teammate Ozzie Smith's accusation that Clark was a "selfish" ballplayer: "This guy was just getting brownie points for his contract with [Cardinals owner] Augie Busch coming up." (Clark has also called Smith "a speck.")

Moving over to the Padres, he criticized Tony Gwynn for acting like he was superior to the other players on the team. Here's why: "He had this pregame radio show. And the guys, including the captain of the team, didn't like hearing somebody talking for all of us when he didn't talk to us in the clubhouse, one-on-one. He wouldn't talk to me about baseball, so I didn't want to hear him on the radio saying we as a team feel this way, because I didn't feel that way."

After Giants pitcher Jeff Brantley hit San Diego's Benito Santiago and broke his forearm, Clark and others on the Padres thought it was intentional: "You know how I feel about the Giants anyway, I can't stand them. Now I just hate them that much worse. Their time will come, believe me, their time will come."

On Roger Clemens, after the Red Sox pitcher showed up late for spring training in 1992: "He brings attention on himself that's not needed. Maybe he had things to do back home. Well, so do I. I didn't want to leave my family either."

On being designated hitter for the Boston Red Sox: "I don't know why I even have a glove."

On San Francisco columnist Glenn Dickey, who quoted Clark as saying 'I don't know why I even have a glove,' among other things, and stirred up a controversy in Boston: "I didn't say it. He's lying . . . Why would I say that? The team is in first place." (Dickey stood by his story.)

On being booed in Boston: "It's an honor to be booed by Boston fans. In San Diego, you'd ground into a double play, the winning run would score, and they'd boo. "Oh, what, you mean we're ahead? Oh, yea!' "

Pedro Guerrero, Wit

Pedro Guerrero is not known as being particularly funny or witty or even outspoken like Jack Clark. But his name seems to pop up now and then in the lowbrow annals of baseball insult literature. There is that well-traveled story dating back to the days when Pedro was a Dodger holding down third base in an infield with second baseman Steve Sax, who, because of psychological problems or some such thing, was having all kinds of troubles throwing to first. Anyhow Pedro, who was not exactly a Hoover vacuum cleaner in the infield himself, had just mauled a routine grounder, sending his manager Tommy Lasorda into a fit.

"What the hell are you thinking out there?" Lasorda demanded.

"Well," said Pedro, "I'm thinking two things."

"Yeah, what are they?"

"First I'm thinking: 'I hope they don't hit it to me.' "

"And the second thing?"

"I hope they don't hit it to Sax."

It was Pedro who said of sportswriters, "Sometimes they write what I say, and not what I mean," and of lefthanders, "I don't like them— they throw with different hands." These are not exactly insults but they are peculiar enough (in a Berraesque sort of way) to merit attention. But Pedro's utterances are not always so full of whimsy; he can let it rip too, such as when Bob Walk struck him out throwing all curveballs even though the Pirates, leading the Dodgers by a big margin, had the game safely in hand. Pedro accused Walk of being less than a man for not challenging him with fastballs and, although Guerrero's exact words were not recorded, the pitcher's response was: "I apologize for the breaking balls. Next time I'll throw underhanded."

Whining, Woofing and Blowing Smoke (1)

"He looks like a guy who went to a fantasy camp and decided to stay."

—Don Sutton, on pudgeball first baseman John Kruk

"Cory will never be able to identify his problem until he realizes he's the problem."

—White Sox GM Ron Schueler, on outfielder Cory Snyder trying to make a comeback with the Giants

"You're going to give it to that little shit? What's he got—10 RBIs?"

—Unnamed Atlanta Brave, as quoted in the *San Francisco Chronicle*, when asked about Brett Butler winning the 1991 National League MVP award

"It's a joke as far as I'm concerned. The way things were done this year, I'm just done with it. If anybody put together two years like I did, they'd be MVP. So it's a bunch of garbage."

—Cecil Fielder, after losing out to Cal Ripken for the 1991 American League MVP despite having a second straight MVP–caliber year

"He's not even in the Top 10 anymore defensively. He's living off his reputation."

—Expos manager Buck Rodgers, on widely touted catcher Benito Santiago

"Donnie's the best hitter, no question. But I have to laugh when people talk about him as an all-around ballplayer. I mean, to be all-around, you've got to be able to hit, hit for power, field your position, and run. Donnie can do all of them except run."
—Dave Winfield, on former Yankees teammate Don Mattingly

"Never in my wildest dreams would I have paid that kid a million and a half."
—George Steinbrenner, after the Yankees signed prospect Brien Taylor to a big contract in 1991. (Earlier Steinbrenner had said that if New York didn't sign Taylor "they ought to be shot.")

"What if Sanders was hitting over .200? Do the Braves rent a Concorde?"
—Columnists Paul Daugherty, on hearing that the Braves were helicoptering Bo Jackson-wanna-be Deion Sanders from Atlanta Falcon practices to Braves games

"We can all feel sorry for Otis Nixon and acknowledge drugs as the insidious disease that it is. Still, when you strip away the emotion, you've got a guy who is this season's clubhouse leader in stupidity."
—Sportswriter Tim Keown, after the Braves leadoff man was suspended for drug abuse during the hot 1991 NL West divisional race

"There's some sentiment left in baseball: To honor a vet in his last season, his teammates have voted to retire the number of his cocaine dealer."
—Columnist Herb Caen, on an unnamed player

"John Belushi in a jockstrap."
—*Rolling Stone*, on drug-addicted reliever Steve Howe

"Let no one accuse baseball of not being tough on drugs. They just gave Steve Howe his seventh lifetime suspension."
—Bill Ferraro, baseball fan

"I don't want some fuckin' cokehead throwing a ball 90 mph at me."
—Wade Boggs, on the prospect of facing Dwight Gooden during the latter's drug problems

After Bo Jackson spurned two young autograph-seekers at the 1989 All-Star Game, a columnist wrote, "Bo, you can hit a baseball far, and you can run past and over tacklers with a football. But Bo, you're also a jerk."

"These guys don't need a hitting coach, they need a shrink."
—Richie Hebner, ex–Boston hitting coach, on the 1992 Red Sox. (Hebner also said, referring to the Sox, "I hope they've got some pacifiers around that clubhouse.")

"You used to be a nice guy, but now all you guys make so much money you think you can get away with anything."
—Ump Eric Gregg to Bobby Bonilla during an argument over a call. (Gregg later denied saying exactly these words.)

"What are they going to do, bench me?"
—Jose Canseco, on being told that the A's were unhappy with him for reporting late to 1992 spring training. (Editor's note: No, Jose, they didn't bench you, but they did trade you.)

"He's a key player and he struts around like he's not into it and not part of the team. It's not good for any of the guys to see that. It's like a cancer on the team. Pretty soon it's going to do nothing but eat away at the team and do no good."
—Carney Lansford, on A's teammate Rickey Henderson moping around during 1992 spring training

"I think it's kind of funny, that he plays two games and then can't go tonight. We want our best people in there. I'm sure there are a lot of people in the minor leagues who would like to play for us."
—Barry Bonds, on Pirates teammate Jeff King, after King hurt his back in the 1990 ALCS and had to sit out

"The world probably could muster some sympathy for the guy if he weren't so damned abrasive. The chip on [Barry] Bonds's shoulder is bigger than Rafael Belliard."
—Jerry Crasnick, columnist

A Matter of Black and White?

Barry Bonds, suggesting why the Pirates signed Andy Van Slyke to a big, long-term contract but not Bobby Bonilla or himself:
"Do you think Bobby Bonilla should make more than Andy Van Slyke? He's worth more. I think so. Everyone knows what's going on with this team. Open your eyes. Wipe those glasses." Bonds has also referred to Van Slyke as "the great white hope."
And now, Andy Van Slyke on why he thinks Pittsburgh didn't

cough up all the dough that Bonilla wanted: "I can't blame the Pirates for not paying him the money he's demanding. I don't think he's worth five-, five-and-a-half-million dollars. I don't think anybody is. I think what the Pirates are doing is financially responsible . . . I mean, Bobby Bonilla is a good player and a good influence in the clubhouse, but is he the kind of player people pay to see? I don't think so."

Will and Jeff

Is Will Clark a racist? Was Jeffrey Leonard a tumor? If you can believe it, these were two of the hotly debated topics in the days leading up to the 1989 World Series. Clark and Leonard were teammates until the Giants shipped the latter to Milwaukee the year before. It was commonly understood that the two didn't get along but nobody knew quite how much, until Clark brought it up as the Giants got set to meet the A's in the Series:

"He was a tumor. We got rid of him, now look where we are. He was a jealous ballplayer. He couldn't understand why a player was called up and got all the attention. So he made my life miserable. I don't want to talk about that guy. The stuff he did didn't have anything to do with baseball."

Naturally, this called for an answer from Leonard, who talked about why the two men had come to blows once in Philadelphia, as well as a number of other unappetizing items:

"I'm going to respond. But I don't know why he brought all this up. This shit doesn't need to be out at World Series time. Whatever Will's reason, it's in very poor taste. It's about time Will Clark came out of the closet. Talk about my personality . . . Let's unveil his true personality. He's a talented hitter, but he's a prejudiced bastard.

"First I want to clear up what happened with that fight in Philadelphia. My nephew approached him in Philadelphia and asked him for his autograph. Will told him to get his black ass out of there. The next day they had to pull me off him in the clubhouse . . .

"That was never printed. They reversed it. They put it all on me. In the paper it said we fought over some balls and Will Clark fired six unanswered punches at the Hac Man. Then there was something that happened with Chris Brown. Will's racial remarks went down all the time. He actually called Chris Brown a nigger to his face. I came back from the Pittsburgh [drug] trials and I was called into the manager's office. 'We have a problem,' Roger Craig said. 'Will called Chris a nigger.'

Is sweet-swinging Will Clark a foul-mouthed racist? An ex-teammate claimed he was.

"We held a meeting after batting practice [to discuss the incident], but they closed that, too, like Will was Clark Kent or something, and they had to protect his true identity. They wanted a white hero, so they had to close it up . . .

"Those are personality flaws in Will's character. I hope by now he's cleared them up." Leonard went on to say that it wasn't his fault the Giants dropped the 1987 League Championship Series to St. Louis; he was MVP in a losing cause while Clark froze up. "His asshole was so tight he couldn't even use the bathroom," said Leonard. As for the charges of jealousy, the Hac Man dismissed that too: "Will is a great hitter, but I'm not jealous. I was there with Joe Morgan, Reggie Smith, Jack Clark, Darrel Evans and Vida Blue. I'm going to be jealous of Will Clark?"

Other Views of Will the Thrill

"There are a group of top sluggers in the game, a small elite that includes Canseco, Bonilla and Tartabull. Does Will Clark fit into that class? I don't think so. He's a good player, but not in that class."
—Dennis Gilbert, who is (not coincidentally) the agent for Bonilla and Tartabull

"Will Clark, you big dummy. I'm making a million more than you are. You overrated, slow, three-toed sloth with no arms. You hear me, boy?"
—Jose Canseco of the A's, taunting his cross-bay rival on the Giants

"I look at his contract and I'm thinking, 'Give me a break.' How long has the guy been around, four years? . . . And now they're paying a guy like Will Clark like he's in the Hall of Fame. People in San Francisco say that he's the best player to ever play for them. The Thrill, he's better than Willie McCovey? Right. You've got to be kidding me."
—Jack Clark, after Will (no relation) signed his four-year, $15-million deal in 1990

Whining, Woofing and Blowing Smoke (II)

"With Pete Rose in the correctional facility at Marion, Illinois, people have been asking about the dimensions of the walls there. It's 450 to straight-away center and 375 down the lines."
—David Letterman, after baseball's all-time base-hit king went to prison in 1990 for income tax evasion

"I felt as if I were playing baseball at Dred Scott Memorial Park in glorious downtown Johannesburg."
—Darryl Strawberry, from his book, on what it was like to play for the Mets at Shea Stadium. (When questioned by reporters, Darryl later admitted not knowing who Dred Scott was or the location of Johannesburg.)

"A lot of these athletes today, they might not even be able to tell you who Jackie Robinson or Curt Flood was. If it weren't for Jackie Robinson, these guys wouldn't have made much money. If it weren't for Curt Flood, sacrificing his career for free agency, these .250 hitters wouldn't be making $1.5 million. These guys are lumps. They don't think anybody ever came before them."
—Spike Lee, filmmaker

"Because of what we perceive as slanderous attacks aimed at members of this ballclub, we regretfully have found it necessary to immediately cease to communicate with all members of the media. We have been ripped apart as a family and we will stand together in this as a family."
—A joint statement by the New York Mets at their 1992 spring training camp

"People may have thought the Mets to be fools for remaining silent this past week, but now it seems they're going to open their mouths and remove all doubt."
—New York Post, after the Mets decided to rescind their boycott and begin talking to the press again

"I don't know about you, but I wish the Mets had maintained their vow of silence all summer."
—Glen Waggoner, sportswriter

"I like to call the American League East the Fortune 500. Because they are spending a fortune and playing .500."
—Syd Thrift, former AL East general manager

"That was no Ted Williams or Babe Ruth they were hitting for me. I want to know how terrible a player he thinks I am. When something smells you get rid of it. I've seen enough. This is serious. I want out."
—Jose Gonzalez, weak-hitting Dodger outfielder, after Tommy Lasorda sent the equally weak-hitting Mike Sharperson up to bat for him

"Robin tries hard, but it's useless. He's just plain dumb."
—*Boston Globe* reporter, on interviewing the young Robin Yount

"I never managed a real God Squadder before. In Texas, a lot of my players weren't smart enough to read the Bible."
—California manager Doug Rader, when asked how he'd handle born-again Christian Gary Gaetti after Gaetti joined the Angels. (As it happened, Gaetti outlasted Rader on the team.)

"It's kind of silly to me, but we're not winning and this is Stick's club. He wants an organization that will be puppets for him and do what he wants."
—Don Mattingly, after being given an ultimatum (cut your hair or don't play) by Yankee GM Gene Michael in one of the silliest episodes of 1991

"Just how absurd the whole Yankee business became was summed up when manager Stump Merrill said Pascual Perez might miss a start because of the length of his hair. Here they've spent $4 million on a guy who's had two wins in a Yankees uniform, spent countless thousands on rehabilitation and set a record for simulated games, and Perez wasn't going to start because of his hair?!"
—Peter Gammons, columnist

"If you're a career Yankees hater—raised as I was in Brooklyn, there was no choice—don't you love it? Is there anything more satisfying in this year of skewed economics than the knowledge each night that the Yankees' top two starters are going to be Scott Sanderson and Melido Perez?"
—Sportswriter Bill Conlin, early in the 1992 season

"McGwire got his 49 [home runs] in his rookie year, before the pitchers figured him out, and with a lot of good batters on either side of him. Trade McGwire to the Yankees, where everyone is struggling, and we would see him in Columbus in a year."
—Sportswriter William Nack, on strikeout-prone slugger Mark McGwire

"He had so much to improve. Obviously, he hasn't."
—Former A's hitting coach Rick Burleson, on Mark McGwire's progress as a hitter

"I'm supposed to write my congressman because a 68-year-old guy can't get one more at bat? I don't think so. It's time for Minoso to get on line for tickets to the Perry Como concert tour and stop bothering us with all this nonsense."

—Mike Lupica, on Minnie Minoso's attempt in 1990 to play for the White Sox and become the first person to play major league ball in five different decades

"Expansion won't dilute baseball's talent pool, because it's already diluted. Kids don't play the game anymore. No one plays the game anymore. Kids who play do it because Mother wants them babysat for the afternoon. When I was a kid, I played because I wanted to."

—Carleton Fisk, sounding crankier the older he gets

"It's not really fair. They say happy cows give more milk, but they've basically told me I'm dog meat. They've predetermined that I'm washed up, that I can't have an impact. Physically I'm here, but mentally I say, 'What am I doing here?'"

—The aging Kirk Gibson, mixing his metaphors but declaring that he wanted out of Kansas City prior to the '92 season; (the Royals granted his wish).

"I don't know how he's on the team ahead of me, but if you can prove to me that I don't deserve to start, I'll kiss my own behind."

—Julio Franco, after Roberto Alomar was named as the starting second baseman on the 1991 American League All-Star team

"I have nothing to prove. I deserve to be there. I have the numbers. He's doing all the talking, I'm not going to listen. He's just another ball-player. He doesn't sign my paycheck. He's going to have to wait five or six innings before he gets into the All-Star game."

—Roberto Alomar, responding to Franco's comments (which Franco later denied making)

"From the list I saw, none of those guys have pitched better than me. Some haven't even been as good. It would have been nice, it would have been the highlight of my career, but that's all right. It goes to show the game is a joke."

—More All-Star bitching from pitcher Mike Morgan, who didn't make the 1991 team

"Congratulations, Denver. With the addition of major league baseball, you now have three of the most worthless franchises in all of professional sports."
—Columnist Woody Paige, after it was announced that Denver would have a baseball expansion franchise to go along with the basketball Nuggets and the football Broncos

"While Fay Vincent is realigning, he might consider putting the Angels in the Pacific Coast League."
—Michael Ventre, columnist

"Waiting for the Dodgers and Angels to get into the pennant race is like leaving the porch light on for Amelia Earhart to return."
—Los Angeles radio deejay, during 1992 season

"I don't like him—it's that simple. He screwed me in Triple A and I think he remembers screwing me."
—Tony Gwynn, on umpire Charlie Williams

"If that's considered bumping, then maybe we ought to be playing in skirts."
—Twins Manager Tom Kelly, after one of his players was fined for jostling an umpire during an argument

"There are only a few good umpires in this league that bear down. It's not right. We're trying to make a living out there and they're just trying to get the game over."
—Wally Backman, after being traded to the American League; (he's since moved back to the National).

"I have no interest in the American League. I have no friends over there or pitchers I have to watch, so I don't watch. When I retire and there's no one left in the game I know, I won't watch baseball on television. Too boring."
—Keith Hernandez, when he was with the Mets

The Difference Between the National and American Leagues

"The difference is like the difference between exciting and boring."
—Mitch Webster, comparing the (exciting) National with the (boring) American

"Hell, every game over there is three-and-a-half hours. I don't know why every game has to be so damn long, but they are."
—Wally Backman

"American League pitchers start you out 0–2, and three hours later, it's 3–2."
—Tim Raines, on switching from the National League to the American

"Why do they have a Manager of the Year Award in the American League? Really, with the DH [designated hitter] rule making it so you don't have to worry about pinch-hitting for the pitcher, how tough can managing be?"
—Larry Andersen

"The most difficult thing that American League managers have to do is maintain straight faces while addressing each other as "Sparky" and "Stump."
—Steve Rushin, a writer

"If you had a relay race between the guys in the National League and the American League, we'd be done before the American League was half-way through its players."
—Todd Benzinger

"In the 17 years I've played in the American League, they've had an arrogant attitude over there. You see them in the off season and they just blow you off. The American League doesn't exist. I went through this in Anaheim [while playing for the Angels], when the Dodgers spread that shit all the way to Orange County. I'm sick of it."
—The now-retired Don Baylor, prior to the 1988 A's-Dodgers World Series

An American League Wind Machine

They were the Four K's, swinging and missing so much they could've started a wind farm and gotten a federal subsidy for it. They were Rob Deer, Mickey Tettleton, Pete Incaviglia and Cecil Fielder, and they were the most entertaining quartet to come out of Motown since Gladys Knight was introduced to the Pips.

Handicapping the free-swinging foursome before the 1991 season, broadcaster Jim Kaat said, "There will be a lot of games this season in which, if a starting pitcher has his stuff, he can use the same ball for two or three innings." Kitty-Kat was right on that one. Whenever one of these guys swung, a tremendous w-h-o-o-s-h was felt across Tiger Stadium, blowing hot dog wrappers around, rippling the flags, and causing small boys to hold onto their caps. Those four guys struck out so much they made Jose Canseco look like a contact hitter. But oh man, when the gods were kind and one of them—notably Cecil, the walking apartment building—happened to actually make contact with the horsehide . . . Look out! Bye bye, baby. See ya later. Adios, mu-chachos.

We admit that the Four K's may not be everyone's cup of tea. "If you didn't know better, you'd think watching the Tigers that you'd stumbled onto the softball game at the company picnic, with a lot of fat guys swinging and missing most of the time," said Glenn Dickey. "Some people find them exciting. I don't. I like players to look more athletic than the guy who stares back at me in the mirror."

Yes, yes. But these big, hulking guys who looked like they could be John Gotti's bodyguards connected often enough to keep a surprising Detroit club in the thick of the race for much of 1991. Forget aesthetics, think results. As their esteemed manager, Sparky Anderson, said, "Isn't the object to score more runs than the other guys?" You betcha, Sparky.

Why Luis Polonia Should Never Become a Girl Scout Troop Leader

For a runt Luis Polonia is a pretty good player—as long as he doesn't put on a glove and try to throw. Yet no matter what he achieves in the game, he'll always be remembered as the fellow who followed in the footsteps of Roman Polanski and did the shilly-shally with an underage girl during the 1989 season. Luis said the girl told him she was 19; the authorities in Milwaukee did not think this was sufficient justification for his misdeeds and assigned him to the cooler for a brief stay.

It would be in bad taste, however, to linger overly long on this distressing event, so we'll mention only in passing what one of Polonia's teammates on the Yankees, upon hearing the news, told him: "Look at it this way, Luis. You're now Rob Lowe's favorite player." Better that we should leave you with the cautionary words of another teammate, Steve Sax, and hope that anybody else who finds himself in a similar situation takes them to heart. "Luis should have known better when she broke out her birth control pills and they were in the shape of Fred Flintstone," said Sax.

How Major League Ballplayers Other Than Luis Polonia Regard Women

"They consider women sex servants, sex objects, and they want you totally under their control. They hate being turned down. If they buy you a drink they think they own you."
—Phyllis DeLucia, one of three women who filed suit against David Cone for allegedly yanking his crank in front of them in the Mets bullpen

"Spoiled, 20-year-old millionaire boys with pornographic minds, sixth-grade vocabularies, and good throwing arms."
—Andrea Peyser, New York Post

"Hey, just give her a million bucks and tell her to hit the road."
—Pete Rose, on how to end a marriage

"This is not an occupation a woman should be in. In God's society, woman was created in a role of submission to the husband. It's not that woman is inferior, but I don't believe women should be in a leadership role."
—Pitcher Bob Knepper, explaining in 1988 why he thought minor league ump prospect Pam Postema shouldn't be a big league umpire

What Ballplayers Do When They're Not Thinking of Sex or Dreaming Up Strange Biblical Theories on the Role of Women in Society

"Going to the theater [for a ballplayer] means lying in an unmade hotel bed and slurping a can of Lite Beer, while he watches 'As The World Turns.'"
—Lowell Cohn

"I don't know why ballplayers like to moon. Maybe it's the only way some of them can figure out how to express themselves."
—Jay Johnstone

For a dwarf, Luis Polonia is a pretty good hitter, but don't let him near your daughter.

My Name Is Jose Canseco and Yours Isn't

J ose Canseco is the biggest and the baddest player in baseball today —and the only one who's had his own 900 number and visited Madonna in her apartment. He properly belongs in the previous chapter, but when you begin talking about the various and sundry issues in Jose's life, it gets a little . . . *complicated.* Hence, this special section on the King of the Bashers.

Jose the Lover

"Jose attracts beautiful women," says Rick Reilly, "the way a dryer collects lint." This is true of all of today's high-paid, high-profile professional athletes, but it's especially true of Jose and his Body Beautiful. Which, of course, makes married life somewhat problematic at times. Jose has complained that people don't show enough respect for his wife. (At a game in Chicago those disrespectful Comiskey fans held up a sign: "BO KNOWS ESTHER.") But there's a significant body of opinion that holds that the only reason he married her in the first place was to win that $10,000 "I-dare-you-to-do-it" bet with Dave Stewart. And what about that late-night rendezvous at Madonna's pad, Jose? Not exactly on the order of "till death do us part," know what I'm saying?

The most bizarre episode in Jose's storied love life involved one Darice Pequignot, an exotic dancer who appeared on "A Current Affair" claiming that she had had an affair with him. She was hurt because all the time they were doing the funky chicken together, she said that Jose never told her about Esther *or* Madonna. "I felt like a

Mark McGwire and Jose Canseco. While Jose is a member of the "40-40-40 Club"—40 steals, 40 home runs, 40 speeding violations—Bash Brother McGwire drives a K Car much of the time.

big bimbo," said Pequignot, who professes to have been in bed with Jose while that old nag Madonna was pestering him with phone calls. "I didn't think I was the only person, but I didn't think he had a wife and Madonna on the side. I told him it was over."

Jose naturally denies everything, and says that the scandal-mongering tabloids are making up all this philandering stuff. "What's next?" he asks in bewilderment. "Will they have me dating Queen Elizabeth? Will they have me going out with a two-headed Martian girl?"

This Just in: Jose Canseco Seen Dating Two-headed Martian Girl!!!

It was just too easy a gag. Couldn't resist. But you know, if Jose and a two-headed Martian did get together, can you imagine what kind of children they'd have? Awesome, just awesome.

Esther and Jose Play Bumper Cars

Esther and Jose have had their fights. What married couple hasn't? But Jose's and Esther's fights are different than most. When they fight they don't just scream or cry or brandish knives the way most couples do; when they fight they use *cars*. We're referring to the celebrated incident in the 1992 off-season when the Cuban-born slugger chased his wife down and rammed her BMW with his Porsche in the wee morning hours of a long Miami night. Jose was charged with aggravated battery, his wife was reportedly very shook up, and the BMW had to go into the shop for major repairs.

It's not widely known, however, that Canseco's former teammate on the A's, Mark McGwire, was charged with a similar car-battering offense last year, according to columnist Mark Whicker: "But he failed in all three attempts to make contact with the victim's car, and the case was dismissed. An officer identified McGwire's vehicle as a K car."

The 40-40-40 Club

Jose was the first—and so far only—ballplayer to hit 40 home runs and steal 40 bases in a single season. But a Florida highway patrolman informs us that Jose is also the first and only member of the less widely known 40–40–40 Club: "Forty home runs, 40 steals, 40 moving violations."

More About Jose's Driving

Jose drives like Batman. He collects speeding tickets the way budget-conscious housewives clip coupons. His jet fuel–powered Porsche once exceeded 100 mph in Miami and the only reason we know about that one is that he was caught.

Among his many automotive peccadilloes, Jose was arrested in San Francisco for carrying an illegal pistol in one of his souped-up driving machines. Toronto columnist Dave Perkins speculates that this may have something to do with why Canseco has a no-Canada trade clause in his contract. "I bet I know what it is," Perkins says. "It's the handgun laws, isn't it?"

The Jose Canseco Milkshake

Novelist Anne Lamott has called Canseco "a Chernobyl-steroid-mutant-from-hell." Less poetically perhaps, Tom Boswell, the *Washington Post* sportswriter, fingered Jose as a steroid user on a television program before the beginning of the 1988 League Championship Series between Oakland and Boston. "He's the most conspicuous example of a player who made himself great with steroids," said Boswell. "I've heard players, when they're talking about steroid use, call it a 'Jose Canseco milkshake.' "

This caused a big flap. Former Reds great Joe Morgan called Boswell "irresponsible." Reggie Jackson said the comments were "a disservice to Jose and baseball." Both said that Boswell should back up his charges with evidence or shut up. As for Jose himself, he said the persistent rumors about his steroid use were caused by player jealousy and that his Schwarzenegger body is the result of a rigorous off-season workout regime.

Jose handled the controversy with the smoothness of a politician, saying that he wasn't upset with reporters for asking him about it. "That's okay," he said. "I can't blame everybody because one guy is stupid and ignorant." He added that they had looked into suing Boswell for libel, but decided against it. "We can't do anything to him because he doesn't have any money," Canseco said.

Give him credit. Jose kept his sense of humor. With the fans at Fenway chanting "STER-OIDS! STER-OIDS!" at him in the outfield, he good-naturedly flexed his muscles.

Dial 1-900-Jose

Jose instituted his now-defunct 900 number as a means to communicate directly with the legions of teenage girl baseball fans who want to know what's it really like to face the high hard heat of a Nolan Ryan or Roger Clemens. It quickly became a vehicle for sportswriters to make wisecracks about him, such as Tom Barnbridge's assessment of his somewhat lackluster performance in the A's loss to the Reds in the 1990 World Series:

"Hi. Thanks for calling the Jose Canseco Hotline. If you'd like to hear Jose talk about his average in the World Series, touch zero, eight, three. If you'd like to hear him talk about his World Series RBIs, touch two. If you'd like to hear the details on his outstanding defensive plays, touch n-o-n-e. Now make your request."

Jose Talks!

One of the things that distinguishes Jose, as an individual and as a ballplayer, is that he always has a kind word for his fellow man. Just ask him about some of the guys he plays against in major league baseball and you'll see what a kindhearted, generous soul he really is.

"Talentwise, he can't carry my jock."
—On Wally Joyner

"Can't run. No arm."
—On Don Mattingly

"I think average is overrated. Which would you rather see, a guy who goes 3 for 3 in a game with no RBIs or a guy who doesn't get a hit all night until he hits a three-run homer to win the game? Would you rather see Wade Boggs get two hits the opposite way or me hit a 500-foot home run? . . . I might strike out four times, but my 0 for 4 is more exciting than Wade Boggs getting two hits the opposite way."
—On power hitters vs. contact hitters

"Greenwell is playing in a bandbox. I don't have any respect for anyone who plays in a bandbox and doesn't have 30 home runs. If Greenwell comes to Oakland he might hit 15 home runs and bat .300, maybe. Boggs comes here and goes 0 for 14. He goes home and bounces a ball off the wall for a

hit. I've hit balls off the end of the bat that go over the light towers in that park. It's ridiculous."
—On Mike Greenwell, Wade Boggs and Fenway Park

"Somebody on television the other day called Clark the best player in baseball. I almost threw up. I knew at least 10 players who are better than him."
—On Giants first baseman Will Clark

Jose as the Next Babe Ruth

Some people prone to fits of fantasy think that Jose might have a chance to hit 60 or more homers in a season and break the Babe's or Roger Maris's record. William Nack says don't hold your breath: "Jose Canseco is the supposed heir to the Ruthian legend, but he remains a mythological creature, a muscle-bound Minotaur. Canseco led the American League with 42 home runs in 1988. Very big deal. Ever since, he has been a frequent visitor to the training room."

Nack says that Canseco "simply has too many pullable muscles. Like one of those exotic cars he collects, he's too apt to break down, throw a rod, burn a valve, and park himself in the whirlpool for a month."

While Parked in the Whirlpool, Jose Talks About the Legend of Ruth and How Much Respect He Has for It

"Babe Ruth used to use a 60-ounce bat. That tells you all you need to know about the pitching then. You couldn't take a 60-ounce bat up to the plate today."

Playing in Oakland

Well before he was sent to the Texas Rangers, in that surprising 1992 deal, Jose was so fed up with the booing and the lack of support he received in Oakland that he asked the team to trade him. "True fans stick with you thick or thin, down or up. There are not true fans out here," he said in 1991. "A player needs the most when he's down and struggling. These are not baseball educated fans. That's the bottom line."

Some people were supportive of his plight, some not. One who was not was A's manager Tony LaRussa. "Anybody who wants to leave you're better off without them," said Tony. Lowell Cohn, the columnist, was equally unsympathetic. "The fans know the difference between a jerk and a guy who deserves support," he wrote, adding, "Did Jose Canseco have to learn how to put his foot in his mouth, or did it just come naturally?"

But the fans came through for Jose when he needed them, giving him a big ovation in the first game he played in Oakland following his outburst. The great man said he was touched.

The Schmuck Debate

On national television a few years ago, San Francisco newspaper columnist Bill Mandel said, "I'm from New York and in New York there is a word for guys like Canseco, and that word is schmuck."

Like all things concerning Canseco, this became something of a controversy as reporters asked him why he thought someone who had never met him would call him a schmuck. "Jealousy, envy, ignorance," Jose said. "I don't think anyone who doesn't know another person should talk about them like that. That's a sign of pure ignorance. It's been established by psychologists all over the world."

It's an intriguing question, all right. Are Jose's critics all wet or is he, in fact, a schmuck? Maybe we should call Darice Pequignot and see what she thinks.

Ballclubs From Hell

A Ballclub From Hell is not necessarily a losing team; in fact, a Ballclub from Hell can win its division or even a pennant. Winning and losing is not what sets one of these clubs apart; the defining characteristic is more on the order of whining and whimpering. And being obnoxious. Or incredibly pathetic. Or simply distasteful. It's when a ballclub gets so wrapped up in weirdness that what happens on the field becomes almost secondary to the lunacy in the clubhouse. There's no telling when it will happen, or why. But when it happens—when your favorite team crashes the gates of Baseball Hell—it can be a frightening thing to watch.

1991 Cincinnati Reds
"Some Dogs on This Team"

Other teams lost more games, but nobody had a worse 1991 than the Reds. They were less a ballclub and more a psychiatric ward in uniform. *Baseball America* summed it up: "From the uncontrollable Rob Dibble to the psychotic Chris Sabo to the unconscionable Norm Charlton, the Reds [had] more head cases than anybody." And don't forget the kidney-damaged bleatings of Eric Davis, miserly Marge Schott, Lou Piniella vs. his players, Lou Piniella vs. Gary Darling, and much much more. This was, in Bruce Jenkins's words, "The Team That Went Nuts, the world champions who turned into a raging mob of spoiled children." Only Schottzie, the team mascot, took the right approach in 1991: She died.

It was that kind of year in Cincy. The vibes were so bad, it was scary just to play there. Gamely coming back from his near-fatal car crash, Lenny Dykstra of the Phillies ran into the unpadded Riverfront Stadium outfield fence and broke his collarbone, putting an end to what was a very bad year for Lenny too.

One sportswriter said that the Reds, who finished above only the awful Houston Astros in the National League West, lost "with all the class of Mike Tyson." At one point in the season Jose Rijo and goggle-eyed Chris Sabo made like Iron Mike and started throwing punches at each other. This was during a game against San Francisco. On his first time up, Sabo whiffed against Giants righthander Paul McClellan and then beat up a bat rack in rage. A little later on, with the Reds looking like patsies at the plate, Rijo said, "Come on guys, McClellan isn't Cy Young." Furious, Sabo made a move towards Rijo in the dugout, and the two had to be separated from each other.

Norm Charlton was another Red who failed to distinguish himself in 1991, admitting that he threw at Mike Sciosia because the Dodger catcher (according to Charlton) was stealing their signs. "I threw at him," said an unrepentant Charlton. "I hit him on the arm, but I didn't mean to hit him on the arm. He'll be lucky if I don't rip his head off the next time I'm pitching." Norm may win points for candor, but not for judgment. "Something should be done. You can't have a player make as flagrant a statement as that," said Dodgers executive Fred Claire. "It was outrageous, totally out of line." Tommy Lasorda was equally aghast: "That's a disgrace to baseball. What if he did hit him and he loses an eye or something? Then how's he going to feel?" Even Charlton's manager couldn't back him. "You can't condone it," said Lou Piniella. "It's just a foolish statement." The National League did not condone it and suspended and fined the Reds lefthander.

Richie Phillips, the head of the umpires' union, has termed the Reds "the whiniest" team in baseball when it comes to ragging about balls and strikes and close calls on the bases. In 1991, when the Reds weren't whining at the umps, they were whining at each other. After his boys rang up nine straight L's after the All-Star break, Piniella blamed the pitchers. "I'm tired of seeing this every night. They keep talking about our young pitching. What's our young pitching for, four years from now? It's time to get our young pitching straightened out. We score three or four, then you look up at the board and the score is tied even before you even sneeze." One of Lou's fix-it strategems consisted of making reliever Randy Myers into a starter and putting reliever-turned-starter Charlton back in the pen. Wild-man Charlton didn't much like it: "They're pretty much grabbing for straws. When

In New York, Lou Piniella worked under an Owner From Hell (George Steinbrenner), and while with the Reds, he managed a Ballclub From Hell.

you take a guy like Randy who had 31 saves last year and put him in the rotation, that doesn't make a whole lot of sense to me."

Jack Armstrong became a critic, too. One of the biggest washouts in baseball since his starting All-Star gig in 1990, he had spurned Cincinnati's salary offer and walked out of training camp in the spring, saying, "I'd rather make $30,000 on a tuna boat." Jack pitched like a tuna and got sent down to Triple A Nashville, where he blasted the Reds from afar: "They have to decide what their agenda is. They're making panic moves, and I happen to be one of them." Piniella laughed off these remarks: "He was just popping off after winning a game in Triple A. When he walked out on us this spring, he kept comparing himself to Jack McDowell. Well, if he pitched like Jack McDowell, he wouldn't be in the minor leagues."

The ever-popular Rob Dibble contributed to the festive Reds' atmosphere with numerous antics of his own, including some spirited criticism of General Manager Bob Quinn for his inability to obtain Tom Candiotti or some other veteran to bolster their rookie-dominated pitching staff late in the season. "Without a doubt, we definitely had enough guys to get Candiotti," said Dibble. "He was a stone's throw away from our stadium. That's sad. A GM's job is to get players. Lack of action bothers you. How can you keep saying we're going to hang in there, with the Dodgers running on all cylinders? We're going to keep waiting, while the division is won by the Dodgers."

Dibble's ire was not reserved just for Quinn or Doug Dascenzo or Meg Porter, the unlucky schoolteacher hit in the elbow when the out-of-control righthander uncorked a 400-foot fastball into the Riverfront bleachers. He saved some for his own teammates. "I've taken suspensions because guys have asked me to hit people, and when I need a little bit of backing, what do they do?" he said on a radio talk show. "There are a lot of guys who don't like my style of play, but there are a lot of guys on this team whose style I don't like. We've got some dogs on our team. What's worse? Me taking three days off [for being suspended] or a guy taking two weeks off? I've seen guys go down with unbelievable injuries. That's the sickness here. A lot of guys aren't even hurt."

That's right, Rob. There was a sickness on those '91 Reds—a team that in only one year went from world champion to Ballclub from Hell.

1987 New York Mets
"A Bad Case of TDB"

Actually, those '91 Reds shouldn't feel too bad. There is precedent for a ballclub turning into a pack of flesh-eating weasels and tearing itself to shreds following a World Series victory. The Mets did it in 1987, after their triumphant '86 campaign. In the off-season everyone but the batboy wrote a book chronicling the team's exploits—and maybe that was the reason they turned into a Ballclub from Hell the next year. They may have all been suffering from author envy. There are only so many spots on "The Larry King Show," after all.

Darryl Strawberry got the ball rolling in spring training after *Daily News* columnist Mike Lupica accused him of being a sluggard. "Who's he to be saying I should work harder?" Darryl fumed. "I work as hard as anybody. How come nobody ever says Keith [Hernandez] should work harder? I'm going to stuff that weasel in a garbage can, see how he likes my work habits from inside there." Because of the perpetual chip on Darryl's shoulder, it was no mystery who Hernandez was talking about that spring when he said, "Let's be honest. I'm not saying he's going to fuck things up, but there's one guy everybody's sort of watching."

In the Mets off-season, evidently between book parties, Strawberry's wife Lisa sued him for divorce, alleging physical abuse. The joke around camp was that she should've told him she was a lefthander, because everyone knows Darryl can't hit lefthanders. In pointed contrast to the well-liked Dwight Gooden, Strawberry's personal troubles did not engender much sympathy from his teammates. In the lingo of the 1987 Mets, his chronic tardiness, his hotdogging, his complaining, his goldbricking could be summed up in one acronymn: TDB. When the Straw pulled something, a Met might shrug and say, "TDB," and everybody else on the club knew instantly what he was talking about: Typical Darryl Bullshit.

It would be unfair, though, to blame all of the Mets' troubles on TDB. Hernandez, the team leader, struggled through a divorce himself and sleepwalked through the first half of the season. Mookie Wilson and Lenny Dykstra caviled about having to platoon in center. And, fresh from his infamous late night encounter with the Tampa Police Department, Dwight Gooden tested positive for cocaine in April and later checked into rehab for nearly a month. Doc came back to win 15 games that year, but his problems added to the sour atmosphere in the New York locker room

Bobby Ojeda's season ended in May when the ulnar nerve on his pitching elbow went on the fritz. This freaked out Rick Aguilera so much that a few days after Ojeda's operation, he began to complain about creaks and squeaks in his own elbow. His teammates were unimpressed. "I really don't think Aggie's hurt all that bad," opined Wally Backman. "If what happened to Bobby O hadn't happened, with the surgery and all, I don't think Aggie would have even missed a start. I just think what happened to Bobby scared the piss out of him."

Three months later Aguilera was still on the missing person's list and his fellow Mets were wondering if he'd ever show up. "If Aguilera's hurt, he should've had surgery by now," said Hernandez. "If he isn't hurt, then why isn't he pitching?" Aguilera replied that he was not a hypochondriac and he was hurt that Hernandez and the other guys would even think such a thing. "The rumors that I imagined the injury are a bunch of shit. Why would I fake an injury? It pissed me off to hear stories that I was faking it." Aguilera won a bunch of games in September after coming off the disabled list, so he had the last word.

The Mets fell into a pit of their own making early in the season—"That's it in two words," said Hernandez, "we stink"—and couldn't quite right themselves in time to catch St. Louis, although they did make a race of it. They finished 92-70, three behind the pennant-winning Cardinals, but it left a bitter taste because they felt they should've done so much more. Gary Carter, Strawberry, Hernandez, a suddenly power-popping Howard Johnson, great pitchers . . . The team had the talent for a dynasty; instead they created a friggin' soap opera on the order of their pinstriped brothers in the Bronx.

Much of the turmoil surrounding the team centered, of course, on Strawberry and his alleged unwillingness to give an honest day's work for his millions. "I've got a lot of guys who want to play here," said the manager of the Mets, Davey Johnson. "Apparently, Darryl isn't one of them." Johnson made this remark after the Straw stayed out until 4 A.M. boogeying at a Chicago disco and then straggled in late for batting practice before a game against the Cubs. Johnson added that he was benching his young star to teach him a lesson. But an outraged Strawberry defended his right to party till the cows come home and be answerable to no one. "What does late have to do with not wanting to play? I've been busting my butt all year. And then he says he's not going to play me? It's not that I'm one of those crybabies on his team who's always complaining of being hurt. Davey's always trying to bury me. Every time something goes wrong, he buries me in the paper."

Darryl's work habits were again called into question in June after the Cardinals beat the Mets to open a crucial three-game series. Strawberry said he had a tummy ache—okay, okay, it was the flu—and couldn't play. Lee Mazzili, for one, was incensed about it. "He lets his manager down, he let his coaches down, and most importantly, he let his teammates down," said Mazzili. The New York writers, ever on the lookout for a good time, then trundled this quote up and carried it around the locker room to sample Met reaction.

Keith Hernandez: "I have no qualms about what Mazzili said."

Wally Backman: "From what I heard in the trainer's room, Darryl should have been out there. Nobody I know gets sick 25 times a year. There's only so much you can take."

Back the writers went to Strawberry for his reaction. "I can't play on a team of backstabbers, guys you thought were behind you and understood you. They rip me and they can't even hold my jock. What I'm saying is, fuck Backman!" Come again, Darryl? "And fuck Mazzili." Then Darryl issued his immortal line about Backman: "I'll bust that little redneck in the face."

If Reggie Jackson was the Straw That Stirred the Drink, then Darryl was the Straw That Got Stuck Up Your Nose, or In Your Eye. Late in the season Davey Johnson got into a tiff with Mets GM Frank Cashen over extending his contract. Evil rumors of an impending managerial purge floated around the clubhouse, and on top of everything else going on you had the spectacle of Cashen going to the press complaining about how his manager was always going to the press when something was wrong. "I'm getting a little tired of him going to the newspapers and saying we can't communicate every time there's a problem with this baseball team," said Cashen. Speaking about his financial dealings with Johnson, Cashen was even less complimentary. "He's more obsessed by money than anything else in his life," he said.

During the season the Met players, including Strawberry, threw their support behind their money-mad skipper. But after the Cards had gone on to the post-season and the New Yorkers had gone home, Darryl changed his tune. Quoth Darryl: "Nobody could figure out some of the stuff Davey was doing all season. We could never figure out why this guy was playing, why this pitcher was staying in. We just used to watch Davey and shake our heads. He'd talk about strategy and double switches, and we wouldn't know what the hell he was talking about."

Adding: "Man, I wonder all the time how many games this team would win if Whitey were managing it."

You have to wonder, too, what Johnson and the others on the Mets thought of these statements, but you can probably guess. TDB.

1987 San Francisco Giants
"One Flap Down, One Mouth Open"

Is it possible for a team to transform itself into a Ballclub From Hell over the course of a single post-season series? It must be, because the San Francisco Giants managed the trick in the 1987 LCS against St. Louis.

The Giants that year were led by one of the ultimate Ballplayers From Hell, Jeffrey Leonard, who once carved the words "Fuck You" on the barrel of his bat. This was the perfect summation of the approach the Hac Man and his teammates took towards the Cardinals in that nasty seven-game series.

In the first game the Hac Man hit a home run and, after strutting around the bases, *walked* the last seven steps to home plate. This was the first of many insults to follow. The Giants lost that game, but afterwards Leonard told a reporter that San Francisco was "a lot better than St. Louis." The next day, Busch Stadium fans booed Leonard every time he came to the plate and chanted "JEFF-REE, JEFF-REE" when he was out on the field. But the Hac Man answered the best way a player can, slugging another home run in a Giant rout that evened the series at one game apiece. Leonard hit four home runs in the series and each time he did he put on an exhibition, doing everything but a Michael Jackson moonwalk as he rounded—*slowly* rounded—the bases.

The Cardinals enjoyed being shown up by Leonard even less than they enjoyed losing. "I don't like him at all," said pitcher John Tudor. "That's no secret to him or anybody else. Some guys you just don't like." Later in the series Tudor would tell the media, "If you guys want to make Jeffrey Leonard Superman, go ahead. He's hit a couple of balls well. Big deal."

The bad blood carried over to the managers. In Game 2 the Giants' Roger Craig called two pitchouts and caught Cardinal baserunners trying to steal both times. His counterpart in the St. Louis dugout wasn't impressed. "Roger Craig's on a roll," said a sarcastic Whitey Herzog. "Hey, Roger called 22 pitchouts in a game against us and never nailed one guy. Then he complained because his pitchers were behind all the time."

But this was Jeffrey Leonard's series (despite playing for the losing side, he was voted MVP). He kept one flap down and one mouth open wherever he went. Going back to San Francisco with the advantage apparently shifting to the Giants, he dug the needle in deeper: "The Cardinals didn't show me anything. We had one lousy inning. Other than that, they were a beaten team." All of San Francisco seemed to take its cue from the Hac Man. Bay Area sportswriters mocked the kitschy Busch Stadium atmosphere and the "sheep-like" St. Louis fans who all dressed in red. In response Candlestick fans turned out in black—black sheep. The power-hitting Giants of Leonard and Will Clark and Chili Davis were real men; the Cardinals were a pack of wimpy, singles-hitting quiche eaters who played on synthetic turf. Nice guy catcher Bob Brenley took off on St. Louis icon Ozzie Smith: "Ozzie has a stylish way about him, that pretty little slide, but he gets too caught up in style." Chili Davis called St. Louis "a cowtown," a remark that prompted Cardinal coach Red Schoendienst to reply, "He's so dumb he thinks milk comes from ants."

But the cocky San Franciscans squandered their home field advantage, blowing a four-run lead in Game 3 and losing to the injury-depleted Cardinals. Though the Giants won the next two, they had to return to St. Louis where they encountered a pumped-up Busch Stadium crowd that was seeing red all right—red as in blood. The man they wanted to hang from the nearest foul pole was, of course, Leonard. He didn't make the cowtown remark, but many St. Louis fans thought he did and they serenaded his every move with cow bells. One fan doused him with beer from the stands. Others threw coins at him. Signs in the stands read "MOO"—a reference to his "OO" number—and "SCUM BABY."

The Hac Man may have been in his element, but the rest of the Giants weren't and their bats (and mouths) suddenly went quiet. St. Louis shut the Giants out two games in a row and walked away with not only the National League pennant, but also the right to crow.

"I'm just happy we showed them and everybody," said Jack Clark, who only pinch-hit once during the series due to an injury. "We showed everybody what professionalism is all about." Referring to you know who, Tommy Herr said, "He tried to intimidate us, show us up the whole series. He can take the MVP. We'll take the World Series." Looking ahead to that series with Minnesota, Whitey Herzog added, "The thing for us was getting out of Candlestick Park. Can you imagine if they had played the World Series in Candlestick Park and the Metrodome? It would have been a disgrace."

And Ozzie Smith, the object of taunts and ridicule from the Giants bench, had his say, too: "What the Giants have done, all series, is classless. They came in here like they were the greatest thing since corn flakes. I guess that's what happens when you're here for the first time. . . . Looks like they came to talk. We came to play."

1989 New York Yankees
"The Devil's Island of Baseball"

Any team with George Steinbrenner as its owner is, by definition, a Ballclub From Hell. You could almost pick any year in which Stein-brenner was involved with the Yankees and it would qualify. In fact, 1973 may be the worst of all because that was the year he first sunk his claws into the club. But 1977 (the year Reggie stirred the drink) and 1981 (Steinbrenner's self-serving apology to New York fans) and 1982 (three managers in one season) and 1985 (firing Yogi after only 16 games), and 1988 (Billy Martin's fifth time around as manager) were all bad, too. In some ways 1989 wasn't a particularly hellish one at all for a Steinbrenner-owned team; it was typical. Therein lies the trag-edy.

Dallas Green began the year as manager. Of course he didn't finish the year, but that virtually goes without saying when your boss is The Boss. Ironically though, Steinbrenner hired Green as a kind of alter ego: a guy who could talk tough like George and instill discipline in a team that had finished fifth the year before. Said Steinbrenner: "Dallas is tough. He's outspoken. He won't back away from anyone, including me. Last year, it was a mistake to put Lou Piniella on the spot. He wasn't ready for the job, and the team got out of hand."

Green got his first chance to act tough and be tough when Rickey Henderson, as is his custom, showed up late for spring training. "Rickey Henderson is not going to run the Yankees in 1989. Dallas Green is. We sent letters to everybody about when to report. Maybe Rickey can't read." But if Dallas had just asked his players, he might've learned that the leftfielder had been late to camp for the past five years. "Has he ever been here the first day?" said Mattingly with not a little sarcasm. "You have to say that Rickey's consistent. That's what you want in a ballplayer, consistency."

Rickey did finally show up, and quickly made his presence known by saying that many of his fellow Yankees carried on like crazy drunks on the team charters in 1988 and this is why the Yankees did so poorly. This brought denials from a hurt Dave Righetti—"Those who live in glass houses shouldn't throw stones. Rickey drinks as much as anyone else"—as well as from an unidentified Yankee who said that there couldn't have been that much boozing going on because Billy Martin was manager for part of the year and he never let the liquor cart on the airplane get away from his seat.

Later that spring Rickey also said that he didn't get the attention he deserved on the Yankees because he was black. "If I was white," he said, "they'd have built a statue for me already." Then Rickey took deniability to new frontiers. He not only denied ever making the statement, he denied even speaking to the reporter who allegedly quoted him. But even the Yankees got tired of Rickey's act and traded him mid-season to Oakland. One of the players they got in exchange was outfielder Luis Polonia, who was later arrested on a road trip to Milwaukee for having sex with a girl not yet old enough for a driver's license.

In May, the Yankees (minus Dave Winfield, felled by a bad back) suffered an embarrassing loss to the Blue Jays, which prompted a severe dressing-down from their manager. "We stink and I told them so," Green said to reporters. "Some of them must have had their heads in Disneyland or somewhere. They didn't play with any life or with any indication their minds were on the game." Upon reading these remarks in the paper, the fun-loving Yankee players dressed up in goofy hats and boarded the team bus whistling the theme from the Mickey Mouse Club. Then George the Head Mouseketeer got wind of these goings-on and started squeaking: "Dallas says we stink? He's right. We stink. Dallas is the only reason we're still in the hunt. He's trying to turn babies into men. They don't like him saying things about them in public? Well, they play in public."

Early in the season George and his manager were a harmonious pair, agreeing on such matters as third basemen Mike Pagliarulo. "Nobody tries harder than he does," said Green, "but whether his skills have deteriorated to the point where he's not going to get them back, I just don't know." Some of the Yankees thought it was bad form for a manager to criticize one of his players in the press, but not Steinbrenner. Matter of fact, he decided to pile it on too. "It astounds me," said Steinbrenner of the struggling Pagliarulo. "He can't catch, throw or hit. He should keep quiet until he can hit his weight, until his RBIs catch up with his age, and until he can play third base like a normal person."

Then came the Charter From Hell. Maybe the Yankee players were stung by the tough love of their manager and owner. Maybe they were frustrated by losing (they were headed for another fifth-place finish). Or maybe they simply decided, What the heck, let's do an "Animal House" thing. Whatever the reason, they tore up a TWA charter flight, drinking like fish (was Rickey on to something?), throwing food, hassling the flight attendants, and in general confounding the Darwinian notion that man is evolving upward from the primates.

Both manager and owner were furious. Said Green: "I told the players, 'You think I don't fight for you guys, and this is what you do. If you can't go two hours without a drink, you don't need a manager, you need a fucking doctor.'" But Steinbrenner thought his manager should have shouldered some of the blame, calling Green into his office and chewing him out for a lack of control. But Dallas was defensive: "I ain't babysitting these guys," he told Steinbrenner.

The Green-Steinbrenner marriage began to show further signs of strain in late June, when George went public with what was for him mild criticism of a manager. "I feel like the principal when he questions the coach in 'Hoosiers,' and the coach says, 'Don't worry. I know what I'm doing.' I hope this has the same ending as 'Hoosiers.'" But Dallas Green was not Gene Hackman and the sniping from on high continued until Green started referring to "Manager George" in his comments to the press. This was a no-no. People on George's payroll do not talk about George that way, at least not publicly. Once George was desperate to talk to his manager, finally reaching him by phone at a bar. "What are you doing there?" Steinbrenner demanded. "Well, I'm sure as hell not holding a prayer meeting," replied Green. The two had grown openly contemptuous of each other.

The inevitable occurred in August when Steinbrenner fired Green, replacing him with Bucky Dent. The press was not amused. "So Bugs Bunny lives," wrote Jerry Izenberg. "Take a good look at this organization. It has become the French Foreign Legion in pinstripes." Added George Vecsey: "The Yankees' managing job is the Devil's Island of baseball. Inmates are to be pitied rather than admired."

Nor were the fans amused. Chants of "George must go! George must go!" were daily occurrences at the Stadium. And, upset by all the losing and the continuous turmoil inside the organization, a number of anti-Steinbrenner groups sprung up around the country, everybody from BOSS (Battered Onlookers Sick of Steinbrenner) to NO BOSS (National Organization to Boycott and Stop Steinbrenner). Their common purpose? To get George out.

But did he listen? Did a chastened Steinbrenner mend his ways and give his next manager some breathing room? Are you kidding? After the Yankees stumbled to a 2-11 record under new manager Dent, George began chafing at him. "We may have rushed Bucky," said the Owner From Hell. "He might not be ready." And of course Bucky would be gone with the next strong wind.

1989 Boston Red Sox
"25 Men, 25 Cabs"

Ordinarily, Red Sox fans might've rejoiced to see the hated Yankees having such a hard time of it in 1989. But they didn't have much chance to gloat because their beloved Sox, although a much better team than New York, were crashing the Gates of Hell themselves that year.

The classic definition of those '89 Sox was this: "25 men, 25 cabs." The year before, the Olde Towners had won their division in an oddly harmonious fashion; this club, said Mike Kopf, was a "more typical Bosoxian blend of egotism, recrimination and out-and-out cry-babyism." But this was also the Year of Margo, which made it exceptional even by Boston's traditionally dissension-wracked standards.

Margo Adams, the former love pet of third-baseman Wade Boggs, filed suit against him in 1988, but the K-Y Jelly didn't really hit the fan until the following spring when she confessed all—and bared all—to a men's magazine. The details of the long-running Margo and Wade affair—so it wasn't just poultry products that kept you going on the road, eh Wade?—were as sordid and provocative as something you'd read in, well, *Penthouse.* And Wade's teammates got splattered, too. Margo reported that Wade said Jim Rice "thinks he's white" and that he thought Dwight Evans was a tattletale. She said that Wade used to call Roger Clemens "Mr. Perfect." Margo also said that Wade and a teammate broke into Bob Stanley's room and snapped pictures of him in bed with a stripper. They called this "Operation Delta Force."

One of the more damaging things that Margo said had nothing to do with sex but with the way Boggs approached the game. The Red Sox losing didn't bother him nearly as much as not getting any hits on a given day. "Winning or losing was never that important," she said. "All that was important was how many hits he got."

The spectre of Margo haunted Boggs and the Red Sox all season long. Accompanied by his extremely understanding wife, the self-described sex fiend asked forgiveness for his sins on a Barbara Walters special, while every comedian worth the name made jokes at his expense. "According to the *Sporting News,* over the last four years Wade Boggs hit .800 with women in scoring position," cracked David Letterman. Fans at opposing ballparks chanted "MAR-GO! MAR-GO!" and in Kansas City a radio station passed out Margo masks when the Sox came to town. Few people in the Red Sox organization could find much humor in this situation, not even after Margo was arrested for shoplifting following her *Penthouse*-sponsored author's tour of the country.

L'Affaire Margo was a sideshow of the first order, but not the only one threatening the sanity of those 1989 Red Sox. They had plenty of other head cases willing and able to help out in that regard.

Oil Can Boyd, for one. In May, feeling slighted by the Sox after they pushed him back in the rotation to let Roger Clemens pitch against Cleveland, the Can sprung a leak. "I'm not playing second fiddle to nobody," he said. "I ain't no fourth or fifth starter. I'm a bona fide major league pitcher. I'm not concerned with the ballclub right now, I'm just worried about myself, and right now, I'm not happy at all." Infused as he was with such team spirit and camaraderie, Boyd had spoken up earlier when the Margo Adams revelations became public. In 1986, upset over not being named to the All-Star team, Boyd threw an obscenity-laden hissy fit that made Red Sox officials recommend that he see a psychiatrist. The Can bitterly resented this, and compared it to the team's treatment of Boggs three years later. "I got to go to a psychiatrist because I got mad. Here is a guy who says he is a sex fiend. Now who needs the psychiatrist?" said Boyd.

Speaking of psychiatrists and who might need one, let's not forget that Roger Rocket was a part of this team, too. The Rocket was his usual ballistic self in 1989, and everyone in the press knows how much fun *that* can be. "I don't appreciate reporters writing about my family and somebody's gonna get hurt one time doing that," he warned. The *Globe* then ran a cartoon showing Clemens dressed up in a white karate suit talking to a crowd of reporters. One reporter wondered if he could ask a question and Clemens, ready for action, snarled, "Do you feel lucky?"

But Roger's boorish attacks on the press are old hat by now; in 1989, he added to his repertoire by saying Boston was a bad place to raise a family. "There are some things going on up there in Boston that make it a little bit tough as far as your own family," he said. (We can't be sure, but we don't think he was talking about Commander

Wade and his Operation Delta Force crew.) Referring to Bruce Hurst, the Red Sox pitcher who was getting set to flee to San Diego, Roger added, "If you take a family man like Bruce is, there's too many obstacles there in Boston to overcome that. There are a lot of things that are a disadvantage there."

Many of Clemens's teammates might've said that one of the biggest disadvantages of being in Beantown was having to play for manager Joe Morgan. In March Morgan called his team "dead-ass" and as the season wore on a few of his players responded in kind. A disgruntled Bob Stanley said he out-and-out "hated" him. Reliever Joe Price asked him to "perform the usual anatomically impossible act" (Mike Kopf's phrase) after Morgan chewed him out for a sloppy performance on the mound. Others in the media were not so keen on the leadership abilities of the former snowplow driver either. Globe reporter and author Dan Shaughnessy said that Morgan managed "like Chauncy the Gardener from Peter Sellers's 'Being There.' "

Shaughnessy also described these Red Sox as "a rudderless ship, full of sailors complaining about salty food and cabin decor while the vessel was careening off an iceberg." With a vacancy in the captain's cabin, some teams might have relied on their veterans for leadership. But on this team the young guys hated the veterans and vice versa. One of the player representatives was a nobody pitcher named Wes Gardner, which Mike Greenwell thought was ridiculous. "I wanted to be player rep, but Richie [Gedman] talked me out of it. Then I find out he named Wes," said the young outfielder. "If I'd known all this bullshit was going to happen, I'd have gotten that job and a lot of this stuff wouldn't be going on. I told Gardner, 'Wes, shut the fuck up and sit down.' He's been on the disabled list longer than I've been in the big leagues. When [aging catcher Rick] Cerone got up to talk, I just hung my head in my locker. He's lucky to even be here and he acts like he's running the team."

The event that probably summed up the season for Boston—they finished a disappointing third behind Toronto and the surprising Orioles—occurred on June 22, with Mike Smithson on the mound facing Rafael Palmeiro of the Texas Rangers. The Rangers had been digging in at the plate and strutting their stuff all night long and Smithson, acting in what he thought were the best interests of his team, plunked Palmeiro with the baseball. As Palmeiro came charging out of the batter's box and the entire Texas bench emptied, only one Red Sox player, Joe Price, rushed out of the dugout in defense of Smithson. The others just sat there.

Mike Greenwell blasted his teammates for this, saying, "We have a bunch of wimps on this team. When are we going to act like a team and stop acting like a bunch of fairies?" They ran this by the comatose Joe Morgan and he said, "A pretty good assessment." And the next day coach Al Bumbry posted his statement on the locker room wall: "When we start to play as a team together, I'll fight as a team."

Well, they never did. Ballclubs From Hell never do.

1990 Oakland A's
"Outlaw Biker Ballplayers from Hell"

They were big, they were bad, they were mostly full of baloney. Ladies and gentlemen, meet your 1990 Oakland Athletics!

Three pennants in a row with a World Series title sandwiched in between is not baloney, of course. The A's were definitely good, even if they didn't quite live up to their press clips. But what team could? Greater than the 1927 Yankees! More powerful than the 1975 Reds! Better by far than the 1984 Tigers! Then again, maybe not.

The A's aura of invincibility, which was shattered so conclusively in 1990, actually began building two years earlier, the year of their first pennant. "The Dodgers have a couple of guys who can hit the ball over the fence like Jose Canseco," said Scott Ostler, handicapping the 1988 World Series matchup, "but you have to let them bat from second base." Ostler was kidding, but most baseball people expected the outmanned Dodgers to be taken apart limb by limb by Canseco and his large-muscled teammates. Well, a team got taken apart all right, but it wasn't Los Angeles.

The next year the A's met their Bay Area rivals, the San Francisco Giants, in that sad, little quake-damaged Series, and this one went according to form. Awesome! Unbeatable! The Hypemasters came out in droves after the 1989 sweep and stuck around until the beginning of the next year's Series against the Cincinnati Reds. Does anyone remember all the phlooey that was written and said about those A's? It got so bad, one newspaper reported a simulation game that pitted Oakland against an All-Star team of the greatest players in the history of the game—*and the A's Won!*

That year, 1990, is a sweet memory for anyone who loves to see the so-called experts take pratfalls into vats of chewing tobacco juice. Now, it's true you can't blame the A's for what the slightly hysterical media and others said about them. But you *can* get on their case for believing all the hype and acting like a bunch of arrogant, kick-sand-

Dave Stewart made his mother proud in the 1989 World Series against the Giants, but it was a horror show for the A's and Stewart the next year against Cincinnati.

in-your-face muscleheads. "A lot of people have told me that I'm a hot dog and controversial, but the A's have got the worst attitude I've ever seen in baseball," said George Bell, then with the Blue Jays. "I hope they enjoy the World Series. I hope they get their butts kicked." This was 1989, after Oakland vanquished the Blue Jays in the American League Championship Series. George did not get his wish that year, but he must've been all smiles the next.

The A's were an unusual team in that they had such a diversity of people to dislike. The Bash Brothers. Showboating Rickey Henderson, who came aboard mid-1989. The Eck Man and his punch-you-out strikeout routine. Dave Stewart and his death-ray stare. "If the A's made a movie, we could call it 'Outlaw Biker Ballplayers From Hell,' " said Bill Mandel. Nevertheless, the bad-ass Oaklanders rolled over Boston like Marlon Brando in "The Wild One" and seemed ready to do the same to the outmanned—where have we heard this before?— Cincinnati Reds.

In Game 1 of the Series, Eric Davis stared down Dave Stewart and took him very, very deep as the invincible A's got vinced, 7-0. But this was a fluke, an aberration that would not be repeated. "What does last night's lopsided victory by the Cincinnati Reds really mean? That the A's won't be able to sweep another series," said a camp follower in the Bay Area media. But in Game 2 Joe Oliver beat Dennis Eckersley with a 10th-inning base hit and the mighty ship that was Oakland began to take on water.

Suddenly, cracks were appearing everywhere. Jose Canseco got a slow jump on a ball hit by Billy Hatcher late in Game 2. It bounced off Jose's glove—clank!—and Hatcher raced around to third for a triple, later scoring the run that tied the game and set up Oliver's extra-inning heroics. Many of the A's were not pleased by what they saw as a lackadaisical effort on the part of the man chasing the ball. "To me it's gotten to be wait-and-see with Jose," said Dave Stewart, one of the team leaders. "Like he hits the home run [in the third inning]. For me it's 'So what?' Because so often he hits a home run and then doesn't do anything the rest of the day." Carney Lansford, another team leader, added: "It really hurts to go into extra innings and lose. We can't quit in a World Series, and if someone here doesn't want to play in a World Series, I wish they'd go home right now. Something is not right here."

Manager Tony LaRussa thought something was rotten too, and that something wasn't in Denmark but in right field. "If you want to win the game, you have to make that play," he said. "That's a ball that has to be caught. I don't think he got a good jump, he got a horseshit jump." But, as is well known, Jose is a sensitive soul who does not take well to this sort of criticism. "If that's what Tony says, it's his problem. If he wants to hang the loss on one play, then he's totally wrong. And it's very out of character. Have you ever heard Tony make a statement like that against one of his players? But then again you always blame the guy who's making the most money, because he's the one who's supposed to be doing the most." A year later, Jose was still smouldering over LaRussa's remarks. "The whole World Series was put on my shoulders," he told an interviewer. "I lost the World Series. That's okay, because I'm horse enough to take it. But did you hear anyone in management standing up for me? Did you hear anyone there say, 'How could you blame one guy?' No, you didn't."

As the series shifted to Oakland an "air of paranoia" prevailed in the A's clubhouse, according to one reporter. Still, there was enough leftover bluster and braggadocio to go around. "Sometimes if you get a turf team off the turf, it doesn't work out too well," said Stewart. "I don't know what's going to happen from now on, but some things happened [in Cincinnati] that just won't happen at our place." As about so many things during the Series, Stewart was wrong. Jose kept swinging and missing, Mark McGwire kept swinging and missing, and Harold Baines kept swinging and missing (David Letterman's idea on why the A's lost: "A hard-of-hearing equipment manager filled their bats with pork"). By Game 4 Jose Canseco and his bruised ego were riding the pine and his wife was carping at Tony LaRussa. Meanwhile, Billy Hatcher kept hitting everything in sight, Rob Dibble kept blowing people away, and the overmatched Reds stomped the unbeatable A's in four games.

Ah, but did that make the Reds the better team? Not according to Stewart, who lost two of the four games. "It doesn't make them the best team," he said, in remarks that received well-deserved ridicule. "It makes them the team that played the best for seven games." Stewart also guaranteed that the A's would be back in the World Series in 1991. Wrong again, Stew.

For their outrageous arrogance, for their egoistic wallowing in all their gorgeous press notices, and for their insufferable lack of humility in the face of complete and total humiliation—these A's deserve a special niche in our pantheon of Ballclubs From Hell. But we'll leave the last words to a literary baseball fan from Berkeley writing a post-mortem in a Bay Area newspaper.

"The last time that the Cincinnati Reds romped over a heavily favored opponent in the World Series, it inspired the book *Eight Men Out*. Given the A's rash of finger-pointing and excuse-making, perhaps a volume chronicling this year's Fall Classic might be 'Eight Men Pout.' "

1991 Los Angeles Dodgers
"Why Does Everyone Hate Us?"

It is ironic that the 1991 edition of the Los Angeles Dodgers turned out to be a Ballclub from Hell, considering they had so many players who professed to have a pipeline to the Other Place. Gary Carter, Orel Hershisher, Brett Butler and Darryl Strawberry are all born-again Christians, but this did not prevent the Dodgers from blowing a nine-and-a-half game lead at the All-Star break and then whining like little children when the Braves poured it on down the stretch to win the NL West by a game. These Dodgers were the biggest sore losers since George Steinbrenner duked it out with those two phantom fans in an elevator after the Yankees lost to LA in the 1981 World Series.

"He whined about the Houston Astros' talent. He complained about the Cincinnati Reds' intensity. He wondered about the San Francisco Giants' inspired attitude. He belittled the Atlanta Braves. Then," writes Bob Nightengale, "Los Angeles Dodgers manager Tommy Lasorda had the gall to wonder why everyone in his division, much less the National League, was openly celebrating with Atlanta when the Braves clinched the title."

The team's sour grapes attitude stemmed from the top. While the Dodgers faced the revenge-minded San Francisco Giants in the final series of the season, the Braves went up against the punchless Astros. Lasorda complained about it, but Houston told him to mind his own business. "To tell you the truth, I don't care what Tom Lasorda says any more," said Astros manager Art Howe. "I put my best lineup out there. We just got outplayed. Yeah, just like they got outplayed in San Francisco." Coach Phil Garner added, "I give the Dodgers credit, but that's what they—Tommy—never do. They never give anyone else any credit. That's why players don't like them."

Many teams use the "everybody-is-against-us" approach to inspire themselves and band together. This Ballclub From Hell just moaned about it. When Tim Belcher criticized his Dodger teammates for run-of-the-mill play and said that Atlanta catching them in the standings might be the wake-up call they needed, Lasorda mocked him: "Belcher said that? Well, maybe Atlanta will win and give him his wish. I sure want everybody to be happy."

In the closing weeks of the season, with the divisional race at full boil, Darryl Strawberry did some mocking of his own. "The Braves? We aren't worried about the Braves. Why should we worry about the Braves?" It was Strawberry who called the Giants and Reds "a bunch of jerks" for rooting against LA. "I think it was real unprofessional for players from the Giants and Cincinnati saying they hope the Braves win. It shows no class about their organizations."

Some people don't like the Dodgers as a matter of principle. Others such as pitcher Ted Power, who came up through the once-fertile LA farm system, have a real grudge against them. The 1991 race sent him into fantasy land. "My dream is for the Braves and Dodgers to tie and force a playoff, with the Braves beating them, 10-0, in front of the Dodger home crowd. Then I want the cameras to focus in on Tommy Lasorda." Los Angeles had a one-game lead with four games left to play, but the Padres scored six runs in the eighth inning to beat the Dodgers and drop them into a tie. San Diego's closer that night was an ecstatic Larry Andersen. "I was going to walk off doing the Tomahawk Chop," he said. "But it would have been bush."

Going into that final series at Candlestick Park, the Giants, who had had a miserable season, were revved up at the thought of playing spoiler, while the Dodgers were just acting spoiled. "If we had a bad year, our team wouldn't feel good if we beat the Giants now," said Lasorda on Friday night before the first game. Ex-Giant Brett Butler said San Francisco was motivated by "hatred and spoiling," while Strawberry, the only player to be named to two different Ballclubs From Hell, was in high whimper. "If they want to beat us so bad, why didn't they beat us earlier, when it counted?"

The Dodgers occupied first place for 134 days that season, but they lost two to the Giants and the title slipped away on the final weekend. Asked if he felt sorry for them, Giants star Will Clark replied, "Not a damn bit."

The Dodgers, true to their baby-needs-a-bottle disposition, griped all the way to the bitter end. Strawberry reflected that "sometimes the best team goes home early," while Lasorda chided the Giants for acting like they'd won the pennant after beating his club. "If they're happy they knocked us out of first, and they finished 20 games out, that doesn't show me much," said Tommy.

Also bleeding Dodger blue was textile salesman Gary Grillo, a native Southern Californian and a fan of the team. Coming into that climactic series with San Francisco, Grillo thought his boys were a lock to win it all. "I'm really disappointed," he said. "When Giants manager Roger Craig said he was going to play those games just like it was the World Series, I figured it'd mean he'd lose four in a row."

Those Men
in the Crazy Suits

I n my opinion, the greatest baseball manager ever was Connie Mack. Not because of what his A's clubs did on the field—although that was considerable—but because of what he wore. Mack wore a suit and a straw hat in the dugout, the same as he would wear on the street or going to the theater or on his way to church. None of this dressing up in the ballplayer's uniform pretending that he was one of the guys.

Why is it that managers wear uniforms? No, really, why do they? Think how ludicrous the concept is when applied to other sports. A football coach in pads and helmet? A hockey coach in skates? What about a basketball coach dressed up in those cute little shorts and a jersey top? Ridiculous, you say. Connie Mack would agree. For more than 50 years he dressed in his civvies while managing his teams, and no one—certainly not any of the guys you'll find quoted in this chapter, today's managerial crop—has ever looked more dignified or at home in a baseball dugout.

Through the Years with Whitey Herzog

"I'm not buddy-buddy with the players. If they need a buddy, let them buy a dog."
—When asked if he ever became friends with his players

"The way we're playing, I might tell the players not to cross the picket lines."
—As manager of the Royals, during the 1979 umpire strike

"We need three kinds of pitching: lefthanded, righthanded and relief."
—After taking over the Cardinals in 1980

"If World War III broke out, I guarantee we'd win the pennant by 20 games. All of our guys would be 4–F."
—Assessing an undistinguished, injury-riddled Cardinals club of his

"If they'd eat a blasted steak or drink a blasted beer once in a while, maybe their muscles wouldn't keep ripping off their rib cages."
—On why his players kept injuring themselves

"Guys, when you're horseshit, you don't have to make excuses. And you guys have been horseshit."
—To that same Cardinals club, after hearing all the rationalizations they'd been making for their poor play

"You've got a bunch of prima donnas, overpaid SOBs who ain't ever going to win a goddamn thing. You've got a bunch of mean people, some sorry human beings. It's been the first time I've ever been scared to walk through my own clubhouse. We've got drug problems, we've got ego problems, and we ain't ever going anywhere."
—Sizing up his 1980 St. Louis Cardinals

"He doesn't want to play in St. Louis. He doesn't want to play on turf. He doesn't want to play when we go into Montreal. He doesn't want to play in the Astrodome. He doesn't want to play in the rain. The other 80 games he's all right."
—On Cardinal shortstop Garry Templeton

"They're doing the kind of drills they'd like to have in spring training. Take 50 swings, then go to the dugout and have a beer."
—On how his players were working out during the 1981 baseball strike

"This means I have to manage the damn All-Star Game again."
—After winning his second pennant with the Cardinals in 1985

"It was a 125-foot quail hit by a 250-pound elephant."
—Describing a pop fly single by outfielder Dave Parker

Whitey Herzog has never been shy about speaking his mind, to umpires or anybody else.

"We ain't got no bats. This team is null and void offensively."
—Analyzing the California Angels upon his arrival as vice president in 1991

"Look, I want to keep him, but maybe it's better for everybody if he goes. I've told the Cowboy [Angels owner Gene Autry] I want him to live for a few more years, and if I sign Joyner, it'll kill him a little sooner. Any time Wally screws up on the field, Gene will be looking at him and saying: 'Dadgummit, how could Whitey give that SOB $4 million a year?'"
—On the contract negotiations with former Angels star Wally Joyner, who left for greener pastures

And Now Whitey, What Do You Think of Player Agents?

Whitey can be blunt with his players, and he can be *mercilessly* blunt with people whom he thinks have doublecrossed him, such as player agents. After signing on as vice president and head honcho of the Angels, Whitey took Cowboy Gene's checkbook and rode out in hot pursuit of free agent Bobby Bonilla, who spurned their never-have-to-work-a-day-in-your-life-after-baseball offer for an even larger one from the Mets. Whitey said that being rejected didn't bother him so much as the fact that he felt he was used by Bonilla's agent, Dennis Gilbert, to jack up the price for Bonilla. "And if he says he didn't, he's a liar," said Whitey.

Whitey got a chance to express his feelings to Gilbert directly when they bumped into each other at a Miami Beach coffee shop after the Bonilla-Mets deal was announced at the 1991 winter meetings. Gilbert, who had known Herzog for years and considered him a friend, saw him in line and said hello.

"Get the fuck away from me," replied Whitey.

"But Whitey—"

"I told you to get the fuck away from me. I don't want to talk to you. I don't want anything to do with you."

Gilbert said he thought Whitey must be kidding. Whitey corrected him: "No, I'm not kidding. You're supposed to be my friend, huh? Well, you're no friend of mine. You used me to jack up the price on Bonilla, and then you lied to me and I can prove it. So get the fuck out of my sight. And you can take all of your players and stuff them where the sun don't shine."

Concluded Whitey: "It's just that I'll never, ever make a numerical offer for any Dennis Gilbert ballplayer. If he has a player who interests me, I'll go up to him and say: "What do you want for this guy?" And then when he gives me a number, I'll either say yes or no. But I'll never give him a number again, not for anyone he represents. I appreciate that an agent has to do what he thinks is best for his client. And all he has to do is tell me the truth about it and I'll understand. But if he lies to me, fuck him."

Other Managers Talk Straight About Their Players

"You are a bunch of losers. All you care about is your own stats. You're worse than a watered down expansion team. You've given up. You've got no pride, no dignity, no guts."
—Jim Leyland, to his 1989 Pirates

"Don't tell me it's a lack of concentration. Don't tell me you're struggling at the plate. Don't tell me it's a lack of preparation. Just tell me you're terrible."
—Sparky Anderson to the Detroit Tigers, the season after their 1984 world championship

"Do I have compassion for him? I have compassion for Tommy Lasorda [whose son died of AIDS] as well as winos and drug addicts. But when it comes to a young man being paid a lot of money, I don't have compassion."
—Sparky Anderson once more, when asked if he had any sympathy for a young pitcher who had been shelled in his first outings in the majors

"It was the most blatant lack of hustle I've ever seen . . . I have gone to the wall with that man. We have talked to him and talked to him. It doesn't take any talent to hustle. All we asked of him was to hustle and run balls out. This was the last straw."
—Indians manager John McNamara, after Albert Belle didn't run out a double play ground ball during a game in 1991. (Belle was sent down to the minors immediately after this, but returned later in the season.)

"I think the pattern that has developed has to be addressed. I told him this afternoon that I would expect him to pitch 200 innings next year. That's a goal he should have—not just go home and fish and eat gumbo."
—Orioles manager John Oates, on frequently injured pitcher Ben McDonald

"Unfortunately, he gave me more gray hairs than any of the guys we sent away. Kennedy didn't have a mental or physical problem but an equipment problem. He needed a diaper. He would whine when he didn't feel he was getting enough attention and cry when he felt he got too much."
—Ex-Padres manager Dick Williams, on catcher Terry Kennedy

"I think you're going to hit .290 this year—but you're going to be doing it in Montgomery, Alabama."
—Former Tigers manager Mayo Smith, giving the news to a player being sent down

A Player Fights Back

Some players don't take it. When a manager dumps on them, they fight back. Their dignity hurt, their self-esteem ruptured, they respond such as pitcher Balor Moore did when Gene Mauch called him "a big cunt." Said the wounded Moore:

"You can say you don't like the way I pitch. You can say you don't care much for my curve or my fastball, or that I'm nothing but a fuck-up. But let me tell you one thing, Gene. I absolutely am not and never will be a big cunt!"

Some Expressions of Disrespect for Managers and What They Do

"You could find 100 fans in the stands on any given day who could call the right strategy at the right time with the exact degree of accuracy as the manager."
—Bill Veeck, former baseball owner

"A monkey could stand out there and wave at pitchers. It doesn't take a genius to manage."
—Charlie Finley, A's ex-owner

"All managers are losers. They're the most expendable pieces of furniture on earth."
—Ted Williams

Sparky Anderson: Genius . . . or Not?

"Sparky Anderson is so full of brown stuff that he doesn't seem like he has any words left over for a basic, fundamental understanding of the game."
—Bill James

"I don't think he's that good of a manager. I don't think he knows pitching well enough. Also, I think players have a tendency to manage Sparky instead of the other way around . . . I know he's been successful and he has a great record. But he's been successful because he's had great teams."
—Billy Martin

"I'm sick of Sparky's bull. He likes to sneak into town and sneak out. He keeps telling you how great your team is and how weak his team is. But he can't hide the fact he's in first place."
—Lou Piniella during the 1988 season, on the classic Anderson tactic of bad-mouthing his team while building up the other guy's

"I don't think Sparky knew my name for about a year. He might have been closer to Pete Rose and some of the veteran guys, but Sparky had nothing to do with a kid just up."
—Ray Knight, on playing for Sparky's Cincinnati Reds when he was a youngster

"I've been 12 years with Detroit and 19 years with Sparky, and I thought we'd developed a bond that was unbreakable. That's not the case. It's broken."
—Alex Grammas, after being fired as coach of the Tigers in 1991. (In his defense Sparky said that he had resisted management's attempts to get rid of Grammas and other coaches for years, and "if that can ruin a friendship, then I never had a friend to start with.")

Some Job Performance Reviews of
San Diego Padre Manager Greg Riddoch

"It's tough when your leader is that man. There's no trust—no trust at all. He stabs you in the back. The only thing you can do is take a guy for face value, and his face value is nothing."
—Garry Templeton, after being traded from the Padres in 1991

"He's full of double talk."
—Jim Presley

"He tries to come off real friendly and have a family-type atmosphere, but I'm working my butt down here in rehab in Las Vegas and I never get one call from him. If [Riddoch] can learn from what's going on, it's that he can't be everybody's buddy. He can't be in everyone's corner at the same time."
—Marty Barrett, released by the Padres in 1991

"The crazy thing is that I thought he was a good guy. But once he became manager, he turned out to be one of the biggest all-time snakes I've ever seen. The thing that pisses me off is that the veterans did so much to help him, especially at the start, when he was a nervous wreck. He asked for all our help. But the more we watched him, we knew this guy didn't have a clue of what he was doing. The guy is an absolute joke."
—Jack Clark

More Comments About San Diego Managers

"Playing for Dick Williams is like being Muammar Khaddafi's chef. Every meal better be good."
—Kurt Bevacqua, who played under Williams at San Diego

"Steve Boros's place in the managerial world appears to be that of professional antidote. Previous manager was a grump? Hire Steve! He's nice. Previous manager let the speed game deteriorate? Hire Steve! He'll run-run-de-doo-run-run. Sometimes he'll run-run-de-doo-run-run himself out of innings, but he's nice about it."
—Bill James, on the man who replaced Williams

"How, then, to explain the hiring of Larry Bowa as manager? Leaving aside the question of inexperience, this guy lacks character like Dracula lacks a suntan."
—Mike Kopf, on the man who replaced Boros

Managing in Seattle: A Few Thoughts

"Being named manager of the Seattle Mariners is like being head chef at McDonald's."
—Charles Bricker, sportswriter

"There is absolutely no truth to the rumor that the new skipper of the Seattle Mariners will be the Ty-D-Bol Man."
—Bill James

"What level have they ever been at before? How can they say that?"
—Sparky Anderson, after Jim Lefebvre was fired as Seattle manager because, said a Mariners executive, he wasn't the man to take the team to "the next level"

Managers We Have Known

"If it's true we learn by our mistakes, then Jim Frey will be the best manager ever."
—Ron Luciano

"Everyone hates Bobby Valentine so much that they try too hard against Texas, and you never do well when you try too hard."
—Unidentified manager, on Rangers manager Bobby Valentine, as quoted in the *Boston Globe*

"Cito Gaston, even when he wasn't plagued by sciatic pain, rarely showed any emotion. Regardless of the circumstances, he sat in the dugout as if he was auditioning for a spot on Mount Rushmore."
—Sportswriter Moss Klein, observing the stoic Toronto manager during the 1991 season

"Bob Lemon's face always looks as if it spent the night in a snowbank."
—Lowell Cohn, on the former Yankee manager

"A cement head."
—Orioles owner Edward Bennett Williams, describing Joe Altobelli after he fired him in 1985

"You must have gagged on your corn flakes . . . McNamara buried this team to such an extent that it is truly amazing they came back. In reality, when McNamara left, the Red Sox were a team divided and he couldn't control it."
—Will McDonough, after John McNamara, who was fired in mid-1988 and replaced by Joe Morgan, claimed that he deserved some credit for the team's divisional title that year

"He mishandled everybody. He mishandled me, Chili, Johnny Ray, Dante Bichette, you name it. You look at their outfield now. You think they don't miss Chili and me? But they tried to mess with our heads, and it didn't work. That's why their organization is all shaken up now. They're firing people left and right."
—Devon White, after Doug Rader was fired as manager of the California Angels in 1991

"Bud Harrelson is a nice man, but the job is taking a toll on him. The last time a guy aged this much in office, Jimmy Carter was giving 'malaise' speeches and trying to corner the cardigan market."
—Jerry Crasnick, on the former Mets manager who, in the days before he was fired, said to reporters entering his office, "Come into my graveyard."

"When you've spent 15 years of your life to work for this kind of a goal, and you finally achieve it, and then you're told you're let go for betterment in the organization, that's a slap in the face to me."
—Stump Merrill, after being fired by the Yankees after the 1991 season

"Darryl Strawberry was quoted as saying the Mets felt 'numb' after Johnson was dropped. Big deal. They've been numb for two months."
—Columnist George Vecsey, on the 1990 firing of Mets manager Davey Johnson

Blacks in Baseball; or Why Don Baylor Has to Beg to Get a Managing Job

"Baseball [isn't] the national pastime. It's white America's pastime."
—Clifford Alexander, consultant to the baseball commissioner

"Dwight [Gooden] and Darryl [Strawberry] would never go public with this, but I know there's an unwritten policy on the Mets that only a certain number of blacks can be on the team. I wish the Mets would just come out and say, 'Look, most of the fans who come to our games are white. It's just business.' It would still be racism, but at least it wouldn't be veiled racism."
—Spike Lee, filmmaker

"On the field, blacks have been able to be super giants. But once our playing days are over, this is the end of it and we go to the back of the bus again."
—Henry Aaron, after retiring from baseball

"The white establishment keeps blacks to a minimum. If you look around the league, only a certain amount of players are let in. If a black player is 10 or 20 percent better than a white player, the white guy gets the nod. Face it, this is just a white man's game."
—Garry Templeton, former All-Star shortstop

"It hasn't changed that much. It just looks like the guys in the cartel use their position to hire guys who think the same way they do."
—Dusty Baker, black player-turned-coach

"I truly believe that they [blacks] may not have some of the necessities to be, let's say, a field manager or perhaps a general manager."
—Al Campanis, then-Dodgers vice president, in the famous Ted Koppel interview on "Nightline"

"It's like there's no hope, no hope at all. Everyone knows they don't want blacks to take over the game. They'll hire a few of us, but they'll make sure they're in positions where they can't advance. Take a look around. Everyone knows a first base coach doesn't go anywhere. Most managers come from third base jobs. So where are all the blacks? At first base . . . I just don't understand it. It's not like we're applying for the associate professorship at Harvard. I mean, I think Jim Essian [Cubs manager] was the worst manager there ever was, and I think Whitey Herzog is the best. There's a whole lot of us that could fall between those two. If Essian gets a job, we should all get jobs."
—Bill Madlock, former batting champion

"Why is it that we have to toil in the vineyards for 20 years to get a top job? Did Lou Piniella toil for 20 years before he got a shot?"
—Clifford Alexander

And What Don Baylor Thinks About All This

Needless to say, Don's not too keen about it. And in an interview a couple of years ago with Bob Nightengale, he let his frustrations spill out:

"You think about [leaving the game], but they're not going to run me off that easy. Right now, I'm troubled by it. I'm very disappointed."

Following a playing career with near Hall of Fame credentials, Baylor coached Milwaukee's hitters in 1990 and 1991 and, after Tom Trebelhorn got the ax as Brewers manager, thought he had a shot to replace him. Sorry, Don. You must've lacked the necessities.

"They never gave me consideration. Ten minutes into the interview, I knew I wasn't going anywhere. When I walked out of there, I told my wife that was a waste of my time and theirs. I didn't have a shot. They keep denying it, but I've been around the game too long not to see through people when they're lying. They gave me every excuse in the book and, of course, told me I didn't have the minor league experience."

Phil Garner, the man hired by the Brewers, did not have any minor league managing experience either—a fact not lost on the proud Baylor.

"This guy not only doesn't know the guys on the team, he doesn't even know the league. Hey, if they had really wanted me to have the job, they would have fired Trebelhorn when we lost seven games in a row three times, and eight in a row once. You know, if baseball was a government agency, they'd be hit all the time with lawsuits for equal opportunity. Baseball should be embarrassed."

Milwaukee did offer Baylor a post as director of its farm system; he turned it down to coach in St. Louis. Hired to take Baylor's place as hitting coach was Mike Easler, a black man. Said Baylor: "They just replaced me with another minority, that's all. They wanted someone to be with [infielder Gary] Sheffield. If they say that's not the truth, they're liars. You get tired of hearing the same thing. It's always, 'He'll make a good manager some day, but not here.' Milwaukee and Seattle told me they were going a different direction. What direction is that? Is that fifth or sixth place? Tell me.

"Really, I don't see where we're any ahead since Campanis . . . It's not changing. Look at some of the teams. Boston had only two [black players] this year. Come on, is that a coincidence? Frank Robinson told me that when he got to Baltimore four years ago, there were only six [black] players in the whole organization. Come on, is that a coincidence? I just wish someone would say, 'We can't hire minorities,' and end the charade."

The reason some of Frank Robinson's players on the Giants and Orioles didn't like him wasn't because he is black; they just didn't like him.

Frank Robinson is Black,
But That's Not Why Some of His Players Hated Him

The rap about Frank Robinson as a manager—especially when he was just starting out—was that he was a Hall of Famer and one of the greatest outfielders who ever lived and therefore remote from the problems that mere ordinary mortals had in playing the game. "He sits in there, never talks to us, makes you come to him if you're hurt," said an unhappy Orioles player after Frank was fired as manager in 1991. "We're out there getting our teeth kicked every night, and you get the feeling he can't wait to get back inside and find out the basketball scores."

Another reason why some people don't quite mesh with Frank may be that he is so damned blunt. His scrape with umpire Drew Cobble is a vivid example of that. After bumping Cobble and arguing with him over a call, Robinson called the ump "a no-good human being" and drew a three-game suspension. But when given a chance to repent for his remarks, blunt Frank wouldn't do it. "I really don't see what's wrong with calling him a no-good human being," he said. "I don't like him and he doesn't like me. So I felt that he was a no-good human being."

We agree, Frank. Don't back down; keep telling it like it is. Just like when that reporter asked you how your Orioles were doing in the middle of the 1990 season: "I don't want to point a finger at any individual, but until recently Bradley wasn't giving us anything. Finley hasn't given us much all year. Cal didn't do anything in the third spot, and we had to drop him down in the lineup . . . Orsulak was going well, but how long has it been since he's done anything? Tettleton has been up and down. Worthington hasn't gotten the big hits like he did last year. We're getting nothing out of the DH spot. Last year Anderson and Devereaux gave us a big lift, running and making things happen, and we really haven't had them around because they've been hurt. When we have had them, they haven't been getting on base the way we want."

Tony Blows His Top

Tony LaRussa is a law school graduate with a reputation for brains and baseball savvy, but he sure blew his cool in that game in 1991 when White Sox reliever Bobby Thigpen beaned Terry Steinbach with a

Baseball "genius" and George Will pin-up boy, Tony LaRussa,
shares a joke with himself.

wicked fastball that nearly short-circuited the wiring in Terry's head. The A's manager roared out of the dugout and, furious at the sight of his catcher sprawled on the ground, picked up Steinbach's bat and hurled it against the screen behind home plate. The incident stirred up a rash of bad feeling not only among LaRussa and his former team-mates, but also between LaRussa and the press.

LaRussa, who later confessed that he may not have acted at the height of reasonableness, accused the White Sox pitchers of making a practice of trying to put baseballs in the earholes of his A's. The White Sox (naturally) denied this, and Carleton Fisk, their gimp-legged an-tiquarian catcher, charged that when Tony managed the White Sox the only hitter he ever chose to protect was Harold Baines, a LaRussa pet. "I've got a quote for you," said LaRussa when informed of Fisk's remarks. "He's lying. Remind him about the time Glenn Abbott hit him in Detroit. Ask if he remembers what happened then. How can I respect his opinion when he goes running off at the mouth?"

Following LaRussa's attempt to create a new Olympic sport—hey, is "bat throwing" any less bogus than rhythmic gymnastics or ice danc-ing?—the action shifted to his office, where Associated Press scribe Bob Glass endeavored to ask Tony why he did what he did. LaRussa made like Dom Perignon and popped again. "You guys have about as much sense as a kid just born," he told Glass (among other things), and pushed him. Glass, who's old enough to collect Social Security, was then ushered outside for the safety and sanity of all concerned.

The press, as is usually the case when one of their own is threat-ened, drew the wagons in a circle and began shooting at the George Will managerial pinup boy. LaRussa's behavior was "utterly unsup-portable," said one writer in a typical comment. *Oakland Tribune* columnist Kit Stier, no fan of LaRussa's, was more blunt. "Any person who throws a bat in the direction of a stadium seating area is guilty of irresponsible and dangerous behavior," he wrote, adding, "When LaRussa loses and can no longer vent his anger on an opponent, he verbally beats up on media members in his office. It is tiresome and boorish and rude." And Lowell Cohn of the cross-bay *Chronicle* said that Tony was getting too uppity for his britches: "He has been pam-pered from the day he arrived here, and his arrogance has grown and gone unchecked."

Cohn suggested further that LaRussa's famous sensitivity—he's an animal rights activist—may have a gap in it when it comes to one of the lowliest and most miserable of all God's creatures. "Now that you've learned how to treat dumb animals well," said Cohn, "it's time to direct some of your well-publicized compassion toward sports-writers."

More on Tony LaRussa's High-Wire Act

"LaRussa hasn't been too straightforward with reporters lately. They sit and listen to his line, leave the room and often say to themselves, 'What a bunch of bull!' Watch LaRussa's high intensity act long enough and you begin to weed out what is true and what isn't."
—Kit Stier, during the 1991 season

"Tony couldn't manage a fruit stand."
—Tom Paciorek, who didn't like being platooned by LaRussa when he managed the White Sox

"LaRussa is the nice looking MBA-type who buys the family business and fires all the loyal employees over 50."
—Bill Mandel, analyzing LaRussa's style of managing

"He's a punk. He's putting all the blame on Jose when it's the whole team. Let them sweep us. I should have worn a red dress."
—Esther Canseco, after LaRussa benched her husband during the A's bitter 1990 World Series loss to the Reds; (Tony responded that the importance of Esther's remarks to the ballclub were "the slightest shade above zero").

Roger Craig and Glenn Dickey

Another Bay Area manager who has had his problems with the media is Roger Craig of the Giants. In July 1991 Lowell Cohn wrote a column quoting an unnamed player who was critical of Craig and his look-the-other-way approach in handling since-departed Giants slacker Kevin Mitchell. The San Francisco manager was mainly upset about the anonymous nature of the attack—"If you are going to say something like that, have enough guts to put your name in the article" —but he had a dig at Cohn as well. "I read between the lines. He wants to get something started between me and my players," said Craig.

Managers often feel this way—that the attack dogs in the media are out to get them. But with Roger Craig, it wasn't merely typical managerial paranoia; someone really was out to get him.

Glenn Dickey is a longtime *Chronicle* columnist and a sharp-tongued critic of Craig's. The two do not speak to each other, and it's not hard to see why after reviewing a sampling of Dickey's comments over the years on the former 20-game-loser turned pitching guru:

- "Craig's strength as a manager has supposedly been his ability to deal with players, but the cheerful grandfather quickly becomes an unbending dictator when things go bad."
- "Craig excited fans and kept opponents off balance with his Billyball approach in his first season. Unfortunately, he kept that strategy long after other managers had caught on . . . He was still using the suicide squeeze in his second and third seasons, when everybody in the park knew it was coming."
- "Craig has benefited from favorable treatment by writers, who have liked the fact that he always has something to say, though there hasn't often been much significance in his remarks."
- "Norm Sherry is the Giants' nominal pitching coach, but a better job description would be 'coach responsible for holding manager's hand.' Craig is his own pitching coach and he believes he knows everything there is to know about pitching, despite considerable evidence to the contrary."
- "Maybe, just maybe, somebody should ask why the Giants' staff has so many injuries. Is it all coincidence? Or does Craig's handling of his pitchers have something to do with these injuries?"
- "Craig had another possible solution to the problem of too many relievers and too few starters: He wanted to try Dave Righetti as a starter. As usual, Craig made his pronouncement without consulting anyone."
- "With Craig in charge next season, the Giants may as well concede right now."
- "Capsule definition of the Giants' problems: Management, from club president Al Rosen to manager Roger Craig, doesn't understand what kind of team they have . . . Rosen told me last year that it was hard to add young pitchers to a contending club because of the pennant pressure. The Giants won't have that problem this season."
- "He is a different person when he is criticized. He complained this week to a columnist who has been his apologist that critical writers 'hide' from him. Not quite. When I was critical of Craig, he first

tried to intimidate me in a meeting in his office; when that failed he barred me from his office. Who's really trying to hide, Roger?"

Yeah, Roger, quit playing peekaboo! In addition Dickey called for the serving of Craig's managerial head on a platter; the Giants, however, respectfully declined to accept the offer. And so it goes.

Why Kurt Bevacqua Will Never Get a Hug from Tommy Lasorda

Tommy Lasorda is baseball's leading hugger. But one guy he'll never clasp to his bosom is Kurt Bevacqua, who once accused Lasorda of ordering one of his pitchers to throw at Bevacqua's teammate on the Padres, Joe Lefebvre. The Dodgers manager took exception to this charge, and this is what he said in reply:

"I have never, ever, since I've managed, ever told a pitcher to throw at anybody. Nor will I ever. And if I ever did, I certainly wouldn't make him throw at a fuckin' .130 hitter like Lefebvre or fuckin' Bevacqua, who couldn't hit water if he fell out of a boat. And I'll guarantee you this, when I pitched and I was gonna pitch against a team that had guys on it like Bevacqua, I sent a fuckin' limousine to get the SOB to make sure he was in the lineup. He's a big mouth, I'll tell you that."

. . . And a Few Guys Who Don't Want Hugs from Tommy

"Every time I'd save a game, he'd want to come out to the mound and make out with me. I couldn't handle that—not with him."
—Reliever Charlie Kerfield, on why he wouldn't want to play for the Dodgers manager

"I like the DH rule because it will cut down on Lasorda's mistakes."
—Onetime Dodger pitcher Don Stanhouse, when asked if the National League should adopt the designated hitter

"A prima donna."
—Buck Rodgers, on Lasorda

"There's so much difference between [Roger Craig] and Tommy. He's [Craig] honest and reliable for one thing."
—Candy Maldonado, asked the difference between Giants manager Roger Craig and Lasorda

An Ump-Manager Confrontation

"Lou Piniella," said Ron Luciano, "only argues on days ending with the letter 'y'." It was indeed on a Saturday that Lou got into his now-legendary imbroglio with umpire Gary Darling. Piniella and the Reds had a horrible year in 1991, and this was another nasty piece of it. The fight took place on an August night at Riverfront, after Darling reversed a home run call on a twisting right field drive hit by a Cincinnati batter. Darling said it was foul, and Piniella—and the hometown partisans—nearly buried him in a shower of opprobrium. (Good word, huh?) Fans threw trash on the field, Piniella kicked up a tornado around home plate, he and outfielder Paul O'Neill got ejected, and the man who made the call managed to escape with no major body parts missing.

Come Sunday the hot-blooded Piniella still hadn't cooled down, however, and he lit into Darling with all the I'm-going-to-rip-this-bag-out-of-the-ground-and-throw-it-into-right-field fury that he is known for: "He has a bias against us. It's obvious. I don't know why that is. But if he doesn't like us for any particular reason, he should be professional out there and call the game right." The Reds manager said that "this guy's just not a good umpire" and called for a change: "He hasn't and won't give us a break. He should get his act together, and now." The reaction from the umpires was predictable, and harsh. Silver-haired Doug Harvey, who was crew chief that night, said, "Lou Piniella is full of shit. Every year we get this type of noise from somebody. The umpires' credo is built on integrity. And I can assure you, the only integrity left in baseball is dressed in blue. There isn't a club in baseball that wouldn't cheat to win a game."

Richie Phillips, the head mouthpiece for the umpires' union, entered the fray as well, calling on National League president Bill White to send Piniella to bed without his dinner, or worse. "The union's position is that what Piniella has said about Darling is absolutely reprehensible and something has to be done. Piniella has to be deterred from this kind of conduct in the future." Phillips did not stop there, filing a $5-million lawsuit against Piniella that was luckily dropped before it was laughed out of court.

The umpires suing a manager because the manager insulted one of them? Billy Martin or Earl Weaver would've been in court every other week if the umps could do that. Tim Keown sums it up: "Just what baseball needs. More lawyers, more thin skin, more whining. But really, did Darling have much of a reputation before? He's an umpire, not a priest or a politician . . . Somebody tell the lawyers to take off their ties and enjoy the game."

Pitchers and Pitching

This is a short chapter about pitchers and pitching. I was going to call it "Flamethrowers and Other Bringers of the Heat," but I have a few items about slowballers here, so that didn't seem quite right. Then I thought about calling it "Flamethrowers, Slowballers and All Those Crazy But Lovable Lefthanded Flakes Out in the Bullpen." That was all-inclusive but too wordy, so I just stuck with the simplest.

The Maniacal Rob Dibble

Rob Dibble always commands attention, and not just because of his 5,000-mph fastball. Watching Dibble is like watching a man threatening to jump off the ledge of a building. Is he really that crazy? Will he go ahead and do it? With Dibble you never know.

"It's starkly apparent," Tim Keown said about the Reds closer, "that this isn't just an excitable boy. This is an irresponsible, reckless slack-jaw who makes a habit of hitting people in the back." Too harsh? Astros front office man and former major league hitter Bob Watson doesn't think so. "I have no respect for someone who throws behind a hitter's head. I know he calls himself intimidating, but there are different ways to go about it. Let's put it this way: His style of pitching stinks."

What got Watson steamed was the time in 1991 the hot-tempered Nasty Boy delivered a message pitch to Houston leadoff hitter Eric Yelding—not high and tight in the accepted brushback tradition, but *behind* Yelding's head. This precipitated a bench-clearing brawl and a

Is Doug Drabek "a pussy" because he throws curveballs and changes speeds?
Hot-headed Rob Dibble thought so.

suspension for Dibble, one of several he has incurred over the years. "Since the Reds are so out of the pennant race," joked one observer that season, "maybe Dibble could take some extra suspension days now to get credit for next year."

After coming back from the Yelding suspension, the very first time he pitched in fact, Dibble ventured into the lunatic realm once again when Doug Dascenzo of the Cubs dropped a squeeze down to score a run from third. Dibble did not take kindly to this demonstration of the lost art of bunting, and nailed Dascenzo in the legs with the ball as he was running to first. "A blatant display of unsportsmanship," said umpire Joe West, who promptly threw Dibble out of the game. "He intended to hurt someone. He intentionally went out to hurt a player who had outsmarted him." After seeing television replays of the incident Dascenzo also said it appeared intentional, an act of malice on the pitcher's part.

Rob denied this, saying it was just an accident and the ball slipped out of his hand. ("Gee, officer, I didn't know the gun was loaded . . . ") Some of his teammates and others around the league did not accept these protestations of innocence.

"When you keep making the same mistake, saying 'I'm sorry' doesn't mean anything anymore," said Bill Doran, a teammate of Dibble's. Danny Jackson said, "It was entirely uncalled for. He's just digging a hole for himself. I think a lot of guys around the league have lost respect for him, including his teammates. I'm an ex-teammate and I've lost respect for him. I feel sorry for him." When he was with the Mets, infielder Tim Teufel was on the painful receiving end of a Dibble purpose pitch, and he still hasn't forgotten it. Said Teufel: "He's dangerous. That kind of blatant action, especially with his arsenal—you could end somebody's career."

Dibble brought more shame upon himself in 1991 when a ball he threw into the Riverfront Stadium bleachers accidentally hit a woman, a schoolteacher. He also labeled his teammates "dogs," denigrated the Hall of Fame credentials of Joe Morgan, and called Pittsburgh's Doug Drabek "a pussy." After the curveballing Drabek beat the Reds in Game 5 of the 1990 NLCS, Dibble sniffed, "Cy Young, my ass." He has admitted throwing at Willie Randolph, and once contemptuously flipped a ball to a Phillies hitter after striking him out. Enraged after giving up a run-scoring single, Dibble threw a bat (a la Tony LaRussa) at the screen behind home plate at Riverfront, and he has dumped a bucket of ice water (a la Dave Kingman) on a sportswriter. What's next, Rob, a live rat?

Actually, Dibble has expressed remorse over his past misdeeds and sought counseling, admitting that he needs to learn how to control his temper. Which is a good thing. For, after all, a mind—not to mention a fastball as potent as Dibble's—is a terrible thing to waste.

Not Wanting to Waste His Enormous Potential, Rob Dibble Talks About His Educational Plans After Baseball

Dibble: "I got kicked out of Florida Southern because my grades were so bad. So I think I might just get myself one of those college degrees."
Reporter: "Oh, you mean go back to school?"
Dibble: "No, with the money I have, I'll just buy a diploma."

Now, Rob Talks About What It's Like to Warm Up in the Bullpens of Two of His Favorite Ballparks

"I think a lot of people from an atomic waste plant explosion filtered into San Francisco. I think they put all the mutant people down there. They hit you with rocks, bottles and cans the whole game. You feel like you're at a carnival and people are throwing balls at you."
—On Candlestick Park

"You're more worried about somebody shooting you than getting in the game and giving up a home run. People will drink a quarter of their beer, roll down the top and make a beer bomb and throw it from the third level. There's no nets or anything. If one of those hit you, it would probably knock you out."
—On the friendly confines of Shea Stadium

The Eck Man

Talking about Rob Dibble and how he flipped that ball to that batter after striking him out puts one in mind of the Eck Man, Dennis Eckersley. He's a classic insult artist of the mound. When he was young and hot and his hormones were raging he'd get two strikes on a hitter and yell "You're next!" to the batter waiting on deck. After a guy swung and missed, he'd tell him, "Swing harder." After blowing a third strike past a batter and seeing him complain about the call to the umpire, Eck would point to the man's dugout and say, "Take a seat!" He is known for pumping his fist in the air after a big strikeout or pointing his finger at a hitter as if to "punch him out." Hitters, as a rule, do not like to be shown up in this matter and many would be in agreement with Wallace Johnson's statement that Eckersley "acts like he's Cy Young out there." Yes he does, but the thing about the Eck Man is that sometimes he *is* Cy Young out there.

Slowballers

"I hate having to stand at the plate and think about three hours before his pitch arrives."
—Barry Bonds, on facing junkball artist Charlie Liebrandt

"Some of his pitches have the velocity of a falling leaf."
—Vin Scully, on slowballing Bobby Ojeda

"This guy [Jeff Gray] is a long reliever in more ways than one. Rick Reuschel used to pitch complete innings in less time than it takes Gray to throw one pitch. Filibusters belong in Congress, not baseball."
—Jayson Stark, sportswriter

"What's more wearisome than a pickoff move? How about 14 pickoff moves? In one inning against the Mets, Jim Deshaies made 14 moves to first trying to hold Vince Coleman. The good news for Deshaies was that eventually, when Coleman finally did take off for second, he got thrown out. But was anyone still awake to notice?"
—More observations from Jayson Stark

"The White Sox's Melido Perez is Hourglass Enemy No. 1. Instead of a number, he should wear a disclaimer on his back: 'Allow four to six weeks for delivery.'"
—Gary Peterson, columnist

The Best One-Liner on the Accuracy of Those Radar Guns Used to Measure the Speed of a Pitcher's Delivery

"Some speed guns have clocked trees going 45 mph."
—Unidentified broadcaster

Other Pitchers We Have Known

"Mitch Williams has walked more people than a seeing-eye dog."
—Frank Luksa, sportswriter

The Eck Man will not only strike you out, he'll show you up after he's done it.

"He's as liable to hit the Phillie Phanatic as he is to hit you."
—More on the wild-armed Phillies reliever, from an unidentified National League batter

"Houston was begging people to take Clancy. If anyone can convince me he's a good relief pitcher, they should put me in some insane asylum."
—Sparky Anderson, on Jim Clancy

"A rotator cuff operation waiting to happen."
—Remark, on Royals pitcher Kevin Appier and his strange delivery

"He ought to be a drum major."
—Unidentified hitter, on the mound-strutting antics of Pascual Perez

"Storm Davis has signed on with Prudential Bache in honor of his ERA, which is so sky-high that when it's announced, stockbrokers scream, 'Sell! Sell!' "
—Tony Kornheiser

"He went from he man to She Man."
—A teammate of Twins pitcher Scott Erickson, as Erickson struggled late in the 1991 season after a strong start

"You can stay in pretty good shape just running laps around Andy Benes's neck."
—Broadcaster Hank Greenwald, on the bull-necked Padres pitcher

"There are the four Tom House instructional videos, one of which is called 'Pitching Absolutes.' Texas pitchers find them useful, as they wait for X-ray results."
—Mark Whicker, on pitching guru Tom House, whose methods have been criticized for causing injuries. (Whicker is also not impressed by the split-fingered fastball taught by Roger Craig and others: "Arrives at 88 mph, leaves at 200," he says.)

"You get tired of him saying 'motherfucker' every time you walk into the clubhouse."
—Manager Jim Frey, on why the Cubs traded reliever Lee Smith after the 1987 season

More Pitchers We Have Known (Old-Timer's Division)

"When I was a boy growing up in Cuba, Luis Tiant was a national hero. Now I'm 36 and he's 37."
—Tony Perez, 1979

"Mike Caldwell didn't have enough guts to string a junior-size tennis racket."
—Sportswriter Vic Feuerherd, on the Brewers pitcher

"When Seaver laughs, he makes dogs whine."
—Broadcaster Lindsay Nelson, on the high-pitched cackle of Tom Terrific

"I don't mind catching your fastball at all. Naturally I'd want to have a glove on in case you might be having an especially good day."
—Dallas Green, before warming up pitcher Jim Brosnan

"The problem with [Joe] Cowley was that he lived on his own planet, and occasionally he'd let us visit it."
—Don Baylor, on the ex-Yankee pitcher

"A migraine headache. A crazed pitcher best remembered for beating himself up after games."
—Sportswriter Alison Gordon, on Mark Lemongello of the Jays

"Don Stanhouse holds the ball so long he appears to be hoping the batter will fall victim to some crippling disease."
—Writer Art Hill, on the former Orioles pitcher

"He's the only pitcher in baseball they time with a sundial."
—Mickey Mantle, on the slowest of the slow, Stu Miller

"The thing you love about Steve Trout is that he's the same whether he's pitching great or he's pitching bad. The bad thing is he doesn't know the difference."
—Billy Connors, Seattle pitching coach, on the retired lefthander

"In my opinion his problem is definitely not physical, so we know what's left."
—Jim Frey, on managing Trout

"Joaquin is missing all of the face cards."
—Gorman Thomas, on One Tough Dominican, Joaquin Andujar

Brief Remarks by a Pair of Hall of Famers on How Much They Admire Pitchers

"All pitchers are liars and crybabies."
—Yogi Berra

"I've always thought pitchers were the dumbest part of every ballclub."
—Ted Williams

Once a Bum, Always a Bum

If anybody still thinks that signing a big contract means that you've got it made as a ballplayer, consider Matt "I'm-Growing-Old-Fast" Young. The way-under-.500 lifetime pitcher signed with Boston for beaucoup bucks prior to the 1991 season and then rapidly wilted under the pressure of all those raised expectations. By the middle of the year his ERA was off the charts and he couldn't buy a win, not even with his money. But when the Red Sox yanked him out of the rotation, he blamed his troubles on the quick hook of manager Joe Morgan.

"It is tough pitching when the manager has one foot on the top step of the dugout," Growing-Old-Fast said after being shellacked in a game and sent to the showers before most fans had even found their seats. "I felt like he couldn't wait to get me out of there." Then he started dishing on the Sox infielders: "It's tough when you have to get five outs in an inning. Then you tell somebody to move [to get into a better position] and you look around and he's not there."

With the Old Towners chasing Toronto late in September, Young came in to face the Yankees in relief. It was a game Boston had to win if they were going to catch the Jays. But Young couldn't find the plate, walking two batters and plunking a third to load up the bases. The call quickly went out for another pitcher, who gave up the single that cost the Sox the game. The Boston papers jumped all over Young, saying that he choked. His manager apparently agreed. "You can't be afraid in this game," Morgan said, implying that the lefthander froze up like a Popsicle in the pennant race pressure. One reporter even went so far as to describe Young in the clubhouse afterwards as wearing a "yellow shirt buttoned tight to the neck." (As in: choke!)

But Joe Carter, the Blue Jays outfielder who was watching the game on television, had the best line. "As soon as Matt Young came in the game," he said, "I knew we had it won."

Who the Heck is Marty DeMerritt and Why Are They Saying Such Terrible Things About Him?

Marty DeMerritt isn't a pitcher; he's a pitching coach, and an obscure one at that. But we thought we'd throw him in because, like the overwhelmed Matt Young, he illustrates how intense the pressure is on everybody in the game today.

The San Francisco Giants hired DeMerritt in 1991 to work with their young pitchers, many of whom had him as a coach in the minors. But when DeMerritt appeared he rubbed some observers the wrong way. "You couldn't miss this guy's locker in the Giants clubhouse," said Bruce Jenkins, one of the writers covering the team. "It was littered with Hulk Hogan posters and macho phrases that inspired the pitchers to 'throw inside.' He might as well have changed the carpeting while he was at it."

Describing the freewheeling DeMerritt as "a shameless self-promoter and a rather immature one at that," Jenkins suggested that he was auditioning for the role of Brutus with Giants manager Roger Craig playing Julius Caesar. "He ripped Craig and [head pitching coach] Norm Sherry behind their backs at every opportunity. Instead of working in slowly, building the respect of Craig, Sherry and [GM Al] Rosen, DeMerritt came in like a two-bit guerrilla and got blown off the map," Jenkins said.

Wow. Used to be that all a coach had to do was play cards and throw back vodka shooters with the manager. But DeMerritt showed that if nothing else, he has the necessary media skills to handle it in the big leagues, striking back at Jenkins and another Bay Area sportswriter who attacked him.

"First, these two writers never talked to me, and they did not know me as a person," he wrote in a letter to the *San Francisco Chronicle* after he left the team. "I'm sure if they did they wouldn't have written those lies and trash. I was accused of everything short of being an ax murderer. The people who do know me personally know that I'm a very caring baseball man." Adding some obligatory praise for Al Rosen for giving him a shot in the big leagues, he concluded, "I wish the Giants nothing but the best and for those two writers, a) be more professional—before writing a story check both sides; and b) lying doesn't always make a good story because it might come back and haunt you."

Roger Rocket Goes Ballistic

From an insults and invective standpoint, the Oakland A's-Boston Red Sox 1990 playoff series was one of the all-time greats. You had Oakland's Dennis Eckersley showing up his friend, Boston rightfielder Dwight Evans, by striking him out and then gesturing for him to go sit down. Then you had Boston getting all over A's pitcher Bob Welch, a reformed alcoholic, with taunts from the bench such as: "Be a man, Welch. Have a beer. Stop drinking milk." With the aim of slowing the hyper righthander down and disrupting his rhythm, as they approached the plate Red Sox players took a page out of the long and boring book of Mike "The Human Rain Delay" Hargrove, intently studying the coach's signs at third base, rubbing their hands with dirt, tying their shoes, spit-shining their shoes, picking their teeth, flossing their teeth, and asking to see the signs again before finally settling into the box to hit. The A's knew what the Red Sox were up to—everybody in the United States and Canada knew what they were up to—and Tony LaRussa thought it was bull puckey. "It's bullshit," he said. "It crosses the line between good sportsmanship and poor sportsmanship."

Meantime, the A's and their fans were playing mind games of their own, pointing out how their ace, Dave Stewart, had consistently handled Boston's ace, Roger Clemens, in their head-to-head meetings. Stewart owned Clemens, or so they maintained. And the Oakland side told the joke about how an insurance man was making a sales pitch to the A's righthander: "I can give you a great rate on all your possessions—your home, your car, Roger Clemens, your boat . . . "

The Oaktowners also did their share of woofing on Boston manager Joe Morgan and the way he handled his pitchers. "They won't have to worry about free agency or arbitration with their pitchers," said Rene Lachemann, the A's pitching coach. "The way he uses them, they will all be patients in Dr. Pappas' hospital." Truth be told, though, it wasn't just the A's who questioned Morgan's use of his pitchers. "Joe is managing scared," Red Sox reliever Dennis Lamp told reporters. "He gets everybody up and everybody warmed up because he's afraid to commit himself to one guy. He's afraid he'll be second-guessed by you guys." And sportswriter Alan Greenberg couldn't understand why Morgan would go to the bullpen at all, because every time he did the bashers from Oakland went wild. "Does somebody in the Sox bullpen have pictures of him in compromising positions?" he asked. "It's the surest recipe for disaster since Dukakis rode in that tank."

The biggest disaster, of course, was Roger Clemens's blowup in Game 4. On the mound in the second inning, Clemens mouthed some unpleasantries to plate umpire Terry Cooney, and Cooney tossed him. This set off a huge disturbance with an irate Clemens having to be kept apart from Cooney and Marty Barrett, who was also ejected, tossing a bucket of water onto the field.

"The Red Sox are a disgrace," said the disgusted Carney Lansford after the game. "Marty Barrett? A coach [Dick Beradino] getting pushed down the dugout steps? They're an embarrassment to the sport I play for a living."

Which prompted this response from a Boston fan: "Carney Lansford? Really big man. If you strung together his hits from the series, they wouldn't stretch 250 feet."

With Apologies to David Letterman, the Top Ten Comments Roger Clemens Might Have Made to Ump Terry Cooney That Got Him Tossed Out of the 1990 ALCS Game Against Oakland

10. "No new taxes." (Suggested by *Inside Sports* magazine)
 9. "Where's my rattle?"
 8. "I want your body."
 7. "Suck my cocker spaniel."
 6. "Hasta la vista, baby."
 5. "I said . . . *Tastes great!*"
 4. "Jesus loves you."
 3. "Cowabunga, dude!"
 2. "Make love, not war."
 1. "What's your sign?"

The Actual Three Words That Clemens Said

"Fucking gutless cocksucker."

(Now come on, baseball fans, where else can you get this kind of essential information?)

7 How to Succeed at a Sports Banquet or Celebrity Roast

ave to speak at a sports banquet or sports celebrity roast and don't know what to say? Here's a simple solution: Steal these jokes. Okay, okay, some of them won't exactly fit your audience. But that doesn't matter. Just change the names and situations to fit your particular needs. Wha' d'ya mean that doesn't sound ethical? Come on . . . Joe Garagiola, Tommy Lasorda and Ron Luciano do it. If they had to come up with original material all the time, how long do you think they'd last on the banquet circuit? And it's not stealing anyway. It's . . . *recycling!*

A Guide to Ballparks and Cities

A good way to start any banquet speech is to make some jocular reference to the home team or better yet, to a rival team or city that the audience despises. Herewith some comments and candid assessments of what it's like to play in the various stops around the league:

New York

"*Yeah, I am perhaps borderline berserk. But if you can get away with that anywhere, I think you can in New York. I think New York understands borderline berserk. I think New York respects borderline berserk.*"
—David Cone, at home with the Mets

"The first two words that Yankee fans learn is 'You bum.' Then they learned: 'You suck' followed by 'Gimme a ball.' If you don't give them a ball, they'll give you a complete sentence: 'You bum, you suck.' "
—Kirk Gibson, when he was with the Tigers

"The fans just brutally abuse you and they have no respect at all for anybody."
—Butch Wynegar, former brutally abused Yankee ballplayer

"You could throw raw meat out there and they'll eat it. It's wild. Wild Kingdom."
—Jose Canseco, describing the atmosphere in the stands at Yankee Stadium during a 1991 game

Fenway Park

"There's no mystique there. They should burn it down."
—Sparky Anderson, Detroit manager

Tiger Stadium

"I'd like to blow up Tiger Stadium. That cat box around home plate is six inches deep in kitty litter. That Velcro grass in the infield is six inches deep. They doctor their field. It's idiotic for him to complain about ballparks."
—Wade Boggs, responding to Sparky's critique of Fenway

San Francisco

"You know it's summertime at Candlestick when the fog rolls in, the wind kicks up and you see the center fielder slicing open a caribou to survive the ninth inning."
—Bob Sarlatte, comedian

Old Comiskey Park

"This is the worst ballpark in the major leagues. The worst. It's an awful place."
—Ozzie Guillen, White Sox shortstop

Seattle

"When the end of the world comes, Seattle will still have one more year to go."
—Dick Vertleib, ex-Seattle front office man

"It's like playing inside the Goodyear Blimp."
—DeWayne Buice, on pitching in the Kingdome

"How can they learn the game? There's never anyone in the stands."
—Ron "Sweetwater" Washington, on the lack of crowds (educated or otherwise) in Seattle

Philadelphia

"Kansas City fans don't know how to be mean. They know how to be mean in Philadelphia."
—Larry Bowa, ex-Phillie shortstop

"Philadelphia is such a bad city that when a plane lands there, nobody gets off, everyone gets on."
—Bob Uecker

"Even if you win a rowing race in Philly, they boo you unless you go over the rapids."
—Uecker again

After Baltimore thumped Philly in the 1983 World Series, Mike Schmidt pulled up next to a busload of Philadelphia school children as he was dropping his child off to school. As soon as the kids recognized him they began chanting, "Choke! Choke! Choke!" Said a weary Schmidt, who got one measly single the entire series: "That's your Philadelphia fan in the making."

Three Rivers Stadium, Veterans Stadium, Busch Stadium and Riverfront Stadium

"What's the difference between Three Rivers Stadium, Veterans Stadium, Busch Stadium and Riverfront Stadium? Nothing, except for the colors of the seats."
—Todd Benzinger, first baseman

Toronto

"Blue Jay fans are out of the game. They just sit there and wait to see what happens. If the scoreboard shows the Blue Jays scored a run, then the fans cheer."
—Bobby Meacham, visiting ballplayer

"It was so quiet in the stadium that you could hear a nun fart in the 10th row."
—Jays outfielder Rick Bosetti, on the early years in Toronto

Oakland Coliseum

"You could graze 300 sheep in the foul territory of this ballpark, and they'd never go hungry."
—Norm Hitzges, broadcaster

Los Angeles

"In Los Angeles, it's in by the second, out by the seventh."
—Brett Butler, on the well-noted ballgame watching habits of Dodger fans

"Living in Los Angeles was like always being in spring training. It seems like you're getting ready to do something. Dodger Stadium was beautiful, but the vendors were too laid back. 'Karma! Hey, get your Karma!' I need the Yankee Stadium vendors. 'Beer, cold beer, buy it or I'll force feed you.'"
—Billy Crystal

Montreal

"I hate this place. It's not real baseball here. It's tough to communicate. Call room service and you have to go through a novel to get something to eat. Half of the people don't speak English. It's like you don't belong here or something."
—Eric Davis

Minnesota

"The occupants of Minneapolis think St. Paul is a woebegone, stick-in-the-mud, artless, countrified, backwater town of homely women and foggy-bottom men. The residents of St. Paul believe Minneapolis is a transparent, overgrown, pompous, self-centered, pretentious collection of glass-and-steel skyway labyrinths inhabited by gopher-gnomes and plastic hussies. And they're both right."
—Woody Paige, Denver sportswriter

"Minneapolis is an outpost of urban rest."
—Twins fan

"This place stinks. It's a shame a great guy like HHH had to be named after it."
—Billy Martin, on the Hubert Horatio Humphrey Metrodome (a ballpark, as Tony Kornheiser and others have said, with "a trash bag for the right field wall")

"Some fans sit so far from the action and so high up in the Metrodome that they have to have their refreshments brought in by Saint Bernard."
—Scott Ostler

And Welcome to Miami

"Remember when Stu Miller was knocked off the mound by a gust of wind at Candlestick Park? We may see the first example of a pitcher actually melting on the mound at Joe Robbie [Stadium]. It is hot. It is humid. And the rains come on cue at about five every afternoon. The Miami Whatevers may go an entire season without taking batting practice at home."
—Bob Kravitz, a Colorado sportswriter, on what it will be like playing in Miami

"Oh, and did we mention the bugs? The bugs that weigh in slightly less than George Foreman? The Lords of Baseball said they wanted an open-air, natural-turf stadium. Apparently the Lords of Baseball have never suffered an advanced case of dehydration and heat prostration while walking down the block for the Miami Herald. At least in Dante's inferno, it was a dry heat."
—More from Kravitz

Cracks About Cleveland

Cracks about Cleveland are a perennial favorite in baseball. Unlike the Cubs or Braves or other traditional losers, the Indians are never any good so the put-downs are always relevant. For David Letterman's "Top 10 Reasons Why Your Team Won't Win the Pennant," the number-one reason was: "Your team's name rhymes with Schimindians." Steve Rushin has supplied us with a couple more Cleveland jokes —the Indians have taken the L more often than a Chicago commuter; they've been bringing up the rear longer than Phyllis Diller's plastic surgeon—and here are a few others:

"I always liked working Indian games, because they were usually out of the pennant race by the end of April and there was never too much pressure on the umpires."
—Ron Luciano, ex-umpire

"In 25 years, the two most exciting moments [for the Indians] have been Tito Francona's TV commercials for Central National Bank and Valmy Thomas's groin injury."
—Bennett Tramer, sportswriter

"The Cleveland Indians remind you of one of those movies that is supposed to be a metaphor for life and the only thing you can think of while watching it is that if this is life, I'm sure glad it isn't mine."
—Bill James

"If the people who run the Cleveland Indians were in charge of foreign policy, I'd enroll in night school and start studying Slavic languages."
—More from James

"Terry Anderson wasn't the last hostage freed. It was Jesse Orosco, from the bondage of the Cleveland Indians."
—Agent Allen Meersand, after his client Orosco escaped the Tribe for Milwaukee in 1991. (The last-place Indians were so bad that year that one columnist dubbed them "The Boyz N The Tank.")

"When you play on a team like Cleveland, what you're trying to do more than anything else is to impress other general managers. What you're

doing is trying to say, 'Look at me. I'm a good player. Make a deal for me.' "
—Graig Nettles, ex-Indian third baseman

"I think there should be pay-per-view baseball, but let's have it go both ways. For instance, if the Indians, say, are playing the Orioles, they have to send me a check before I watch."
—Mike Lupica

And since Cleveland is not exactly Paris, the city comes in for some bashing as well:

"The place where elephants go to die."
—Ron Luciano

"I went through Cleveland one day and it was closed."
—Jay Johnstone

"The A's leave after this game for Cleveland. It was only by a 13–12 vote that they decided to go."
—Lon Simmons, A's broadcaster

And let's not forget the home of the Indians, Municipal Stadium, the place Doug Jones described as "a museum of unnatural history":

"There's nothing wrong with the stadium that a case of dynamite wouldn't cure."
—Mike Hargrove, ex–Indian player-turned-manager

More Cub Jokes in One Place Than You'll Find Anywhere Else

Cub insults were hot for a while. Lately they seem to have faded a bit. It has to do with how well they're doing; if the Cubs are up, a joke about their lack of prowess on the baseball field doesn't make much sense. But when the Cubs aren't doing so well (unfortunately for their fans, this is the more normal state of affairs) the jokes come back in fashion.

"The Cubs were taking batting practice, and the pitching machine threw a no-hitter."
—Radio deejay

"The only bad thing about being released by the Cubs is they made me keep my season tickets."
—Ken Reitz, ex-Cubs third baseman

"When you play with the Cubs, it's like playing with heavy shoes on. I had to be de-Cubbed."
—The heavy-footed Pete LaCock, upon leaving the Cubs

"When we were kids we used to go to the circus all the time—only we called it Wrigley Field."
—Tom Dreesen, comedian

"Other teams won and made it look easy. The Cubs lost and made it look hard."
—David Brinkley, television commentator

"My latest diet is better than the Pritikin Diet. You eat only when the Cubs win."
—George Shearing, pianist

"How about the new Cubs soup? Two sips and then you choke."
—Popular joke

"Too many guys from 1908 were still on the roster."
—David Letterman, speculating on why the Cubs lost the 1989 National League playoffs to the Giants

"There's no off-season in Chicago. It's only when the teams start playing that the fans lose interest."
—Columnist Steve Daley, on both the Cubs and the cross-town White Sox

Braves Baseball

Until the arrival of Messrs. Justice, Gant, Avery, Glavine, Pendleton, et al, the Atlanta Braves were the laughingstock of baseball. People told Atlanta Brave jokes the way they tell Dan Quayle jokes. Did you hear the one about the Brave player who was so anxious to improve his game that he injected himself with cork and filled his bat with steroids? You say you've heard that one? Well, what about the three Braves who were so despondent over losing that they decided to become junkies. One Brave shot himself up with heroin and passed the needle to his teammate, who did the same thing and then handed it on to the third Brave. But this one was reluctant to take it. "Hey," he said, "aren't you guys afraid of getting AIDS?" "Hell no," said the other two, "we're wearing condoms."

Hank Greenwald, the Giants broadcaster, surveyed the standings in the National League West and said, "The Atlanta Braves are in last place, where they've been for the past four years. I wonder: Did they sign a lease?" Another Hank, last name Kersch, observed that in eight years the Braves went from being America's Team (they won the NL West in 1982) to America's Travesty, finishing dead last in 1990. Of course, the next year they almost won the whole banana, so there may be hope for other perennial losers like the Padres, Expos, Mariners and Indians. Did I say the Indians? Nah, there's no hope for the Indians.

Back a few years ago, when the Oakland A's were being compared to the 1927 Yankees and the Braves were playing like the 1961 Mets, Bill Tammeus used the two teams to explain world affairs: "Some Americans don't grasp what it's been like to merge East and West Germany. Well, imagine merging the Oakland A's with the Atlanta Braves." Or how about this line, circa 1990: "What do the unbeaten 1972 Miami Dolphins have in common with the Braves? One win a week."

During all those years of losing in Atlanta, one thing remained constant: the unwavering support of their fans. Not really. But at least they kept their sense of humor. At the start of the '91 season, just before greatness struck, the Braves held a contest among their fans to see who could come up with the best slogan to commemorate the team's 25th year in Atlanta. Paul Hagen provided us with some of the entries:

- Braves Baseball: At Least the Hot Dogs Don't Stink.
- Braves Baseball: At Least the Beer's Still Cold.
- Braves Baseball: It Beats Getting Tattooed With a Jackhammer, Unless It's a Doubleheader.

And, What the Heck, Let's Beat Up on San Diego While We're at It

"After nearly 12 years of floundering and drift, the Padres are where they are today because they've never had a sensible plan to get them anyplace but. They've had as many rings as Barnum & Bailey, with three people cracking whips at the same time . . . So who's in charge? Lord knows."

—William Nack, sportswriter, circa 1980

"Rooting for the San Diego Padres is like rooting for Iraq. They might win one every once in a while, but you know in the end they're going to get crushed."
—Steve Cozzens, columnist, 1991

"Some of the beach people in San Diego still cheer pop flies."
—Jay Johnstone, former Padre

"We've got a whole bunch of new players. But I don't think they're the right ones."
—Ozzie Smith, assessing a Padres club he was on

"We play like King Kong one day and like Fay Wray the next."
—Terry Kennedy, on another woeful Padres club

Good Lines About Bad Teams

"We're so bad right now that for us back-to-back home runs means one today and another one tomorrow."
—Earl Weaver, managing the Orioles

"We need two more players to take us over the top: Babe Ruth and Lou Gehrig."
—Reliever Don Carmen, sizing up the needs of a bad Phillies club. (This is a variation on an old line, but it still works.)

"The Yankees are four players away from contention—and the four players are named Mickey, Babe, Lou and Yogi."
—Bill Robinson, in a variation on the same line

"At the rate we're going, a two-out walk is a rally."
—Manager Stump Merrill, on those same Yankees

"If there was a new way to lose, we would discover it. We had a lot of triple threat men: slip, fumble and fall. They talk about Pearl Harbor being something; they should have seen the '52 Pirates. We were so bad, they wouldn't put our pictures on bubble gum cards. George Metkovich, our first baseman, would holler at the umpires: 'For Pete's sake, grab a glove and help me out.'"
—Joe Garagiola, a catcher on that team

Garagiola, speaking about that same Pirates club, at a banquet in 1952: "We may not be very high in the standings, and we don't win many games, but you've got to admit we play some interesting baseball."

A heckler in the audience: "Why don't you play some dull games and win a few?"

"If there was a league in this nation that that team could have won in, it has not been brought to my attention. And that includes the Little League."
—Paul Richards, on a terrible White Sox team

"They can't beat any team whose nickname ends in 's'."
—Columnist Mike Penner, on the 1991 California Angels

"The title of the Phils' 1984 highlights film is: 'Follow Us.' Where? Right over a cliff?"
—Bill Conlin, Philadelphia columnist

"That's like a muscle twitch on a cadaver."
—Orioles owner Edward Bennett Williams, after his second-division team went on a small win streak

"The truth is, the Mets just aren't a very good team. Even worse, they lack an identity. The team color should be beige."
—Columnist Jerry Crasnick, on a Mets club of recent vintage

"There isn't any chemistry, it's just inert gas."
—Oakland GM Sandy Alderson, when asked if a struggling A's team lacked "chemistry"

"They say baseball is our national pastime—and what the Montreal Expos play is pretty popular, too!"
—Old joke (that should probably be retired)

"I don't know which was worse—watching this game or playing in it."
—Catcher Terry Kennedy, after a bad game by the Orioles

"It's like they started off historically bad and then went into a slump."
—Broadcaster Jon Miller, on the 1988 Baltimore Orioles (which lost its first 21 games and then went downhill from there)

"The Royals did not play today; they were rained out. They're holding a victory celebration."
—Jon Miller again, this time talking about the 1-11 Royals early in the 1992 season

Good Lines About Bad Hitters

"Baseball is supposed to be a noncontact sport, but our hitters seem to be taking it literally."
—Larry Doughty, Pirates GM, on his club

"That's the first pitcher he's hit all year."
—A sportswriter's wisecrack after Giants outfielder Tracy Jones banged into the Christy Mathewson sign on the fence at Candlestick park while chasing a fly ball

"When you come up, the left fielder takes a cigarette break."
—Oscar Gamble to an aging Lou Piniella, who was having trouble pulling the ball as he got older

"Rick Miller couldn't hit a home run if he were standing on second base."
—Don Zimmer, on the former Red Sox outfielder

"All I'd have to do is make my head look like a slider, and he'd miss it."
—Pitcher Jim Colborn, on being told that an angry Aurelio Rodriguez was threatening to hit him over the head with a bat. (Colborn had beaned him with a pitch.)

Good Lines About Bad Fielders

"When you field a ball, it sounds like Big Ben at 1 o'clock—Bong!
—Rollie Fingers, to A's teammate Reggie Jackson

"Cliff Johnson had the defensive skills of the Lincoln Tunnel."
—Ron Luciano

"He's a Williams–type player. He bats like Ted and fields like Esther."
—Sportswriter, on Dick "Dr. Strangeglove" Stuart

"The Tigers are putting Rocky Colavito into left field because he has the feet for it."
—Larry Middlemas, sportswriter

"The Mets will have 21 giveaway dates this season, not counting games Howard Johnson starts at third base."
—*Spy* magazine, on the error-prone fielder

"Oscar Gamble hits as if he's worth his $450,000 salary. But he plays the field as if he were carrying the full bulging amount in his uniform."
—Pete Axthelm, late 1970s

"Because you're a .399 fielder."
—Cardinal manager Billy Southworth to rookie Don Padgett, when Padgett asked why he was sitting on the bench when he was hitting .400

"Some of our fielders must be allergic to the ball."
—Pitcher Dick Drago, on his poor-fielding Boston teammates

"Jorge Orta never got acquainted with his glove, and he never met a ground ball he liked."
—Paul Richards

Question: *"If the Dodgers start an infield of Guerrero, Anderson, Sax and Brock, with Oliver in left field and Marshall in right, what's your advice to their opponents?"*
Answer: *"Hit it fair."*
—Mike Downey, columnist

"The Astros second-baseman, using the term loosely, is Art Howe. Last year Howe hit extremely well, and pivoted on the double play almost as well as Bobby Doerr. Doerr was one of the greatest pivot men ever, but he is now 61 and he gave up the game years ago, when he began to pivot like Art Howe."
—Bill James

"Now he has to bend over to field ground balls."
—Scott Ostler, on why Luis Polonia was mad about not being able to use an oversized glove

Good Lines About Bad Pitching

"Sounds like an apt description of the Padres pitching staff."
—Tim McCarver, upon hearing that the favorite book of San Diego manager Steve Boros was A Farewell to Arms

"By the way, you, too, can be a Phillies reliever. All you need is an arm, a baseball and a masochistic bent. The Giants weren't about to say anything unfavorable about the Phillies pitchers, but they did pass out bats to each player as he came off the field at the end of every inning."
—Tim Keown, describing a game in which the Giants hammered Phillie pitching for 17 runs

"Our hitters had no chance to bat against our pitchers."
—Fresco Thompson, explaining why an old-time Phillies team finished last

Pitcher Lloyd Brown, after giving up a game-winning home run to Jimmie Foxx: "That's the last time you'll ever do that to me, Foxx."
Jimmie Foxx: "Why? Are you quitting the league?"

Quick-Witted Lines About Slow-Footed Guys . . .

"He looks like a greyhound, but he runs like a bus."
—George Brett, on Royals teammate Jamie Quirk

"How can anyone who runs as slow as you pull a muscle?"
—Pete Rose, to Reds teammate Tony Perez

"He runs too long in one place. He's got a lot of up and down, but not much forward."
—Dizzy Dean, on a plodding Gashouse Gang teammate

"Ken Singleton is so slow he couldn't tag up from third on a fly to Green Bay."
—Sportswriter, commenting as the lumbering Orioles outfielder stood on third base during a game in Milwaukee

"If you prefer baseball in slow motion, don't miss George Foster chasing a double into the left field corner."
—Charles Bricker, sportswriter

"He's so slow that you could take sequence photos of him with a Polaroid camera."
—Ron Luciano, on lead-footed John Mayberry

"When I watch Smalley playing shortstop, I think of those old movies [like] The Mummy. You know, when the guy is wrapped up with all those bandages and walks so stiff he can hardly move. That's my shortstop. The mummy."
—Yankee manager Clyde King, on shortstop Roy Smalley (the same ballplayer, said Mike Royko, "who led the league in the number of vendors struck by balls thrown toward first base").

"Whoever first called ex–Cleveland Indian Mike Hargrove the Human Rain Delay obviously never saw Dave Parker's home run trot. Slow? Tumbleweeds roll up hills faster."
—Unidentified sportswriter

. . . And Bad Baserunners

"He's one of those guys where, if you're a first base coach, you say, 'Gimme a lasso.' "
—Tony Kubek, on the baserunning abilities of Steve "Psycho" Lyons

"He just runs until he is out."
—Sportswriter Tim Sullivan, after watching Chris Sabo get thrown out trying to stretch an obvious single into a double

Little Guys

"His shoes are so small he can't even give them away to Little Leaguers."
—Jay Johnstone, on the tiny feet of outfielder Brett Butler

"One day Dave Parker asked me if I wanted to go golfing with him. I was excited that Dave Parker would even talk to me. I find out, the reason he wanted to go play golf was to use me as a tee."
—Mike Gallego, peanut-sized infielder

"I love to warm up with him because he makes me feel like I'm throwing downhill."
—Rocky Bridges, on playing catch with tiny outfielder Albie Pearson (who, it was said, "ran the bases like a toy terrier")

"Donald Davidson would've been an outstanding major league shortstop, but the grounders kept going over his head."
—Joe Sambito, at a mid-eighties roast for the four-foot-tall Astros front office man. (At the same $100-a-plate dinner, Warren Spahn said, "If we were roasting anybody else, we would have had to pay $150.")

After California lost to Milwaukee in the 1982 League Championship Series, Angels manager Gene Mauch was addressing his players and some front office personnel in the despondent team's locker room.

"I can't do anything right," said Mauch, the disappointment showing in his voice. "You guys gave me a two-game lead and I blew it. I can't manage, I can't handle a pitching staff, and I'm too short."

At which point a voice in the back of the room called out, "No, I don't think you're too short."

Tubbies

"They say Sid Fernandez has lost weight. Wow, he looks like he's all the way down to 289."
—Bruce Jenkins, observing the Mets lefthander in the spring of 1992

"A fat tub of goo . . . The fattest man in professional sports."
—David Letterman, on former journeyman lefthander Terry Forster. (A running gag on the show some years back, Forster finally appeared with Letterman, but not until they had the studio floor reinforced, according to the host.)

"He still looks like a guy trying to conceal a ham beneath his shirt."
—Gary Peterson, on the paunch of shortstop Jose Uribe

"I saw Tommy Lasorda last Thanksgiving in New York. He was a blimp in the Macy's parade."
—Steve Sax, on his former manager before he became an Ultra Slim–Fast pitchman

"Did you hear what happened? Tommy was lying on the beach in Santa Monica and Greenpeace tried to roll him back in the water."
—More from Sax on Lasorda

Gimps

"Some guys check into a hotel and want a room with a view, a room on a low floor in case of a fire, things like that. Bill Buckner asks for a room next to an ice machine."
—Joe Garagiola, on the gimp-kneed first baseman

"Kirk Gibson isn't in the AL or the NL. He's a permanent member of the DL."
—Steve Rushin, sportswriter

"Don Robinson hopes to become the first reliever wheelbarrowed in from the bullpen."
—Tony Kornheiser, on the oft-injured journeyman pitcher

Geezers

"This guy is so old that the first time he had athlete's foot, it was Absorbine Sr."
—Bob Costas, on the 45-year-old Tommy John

Player-turned-broadcaster Ron Santo: "In my day, we didn't have these fancy training aids, like magnetic resonance imaging."
Bob Brenley: "In your day, they were still using leeches."

"I'm not surprised at the big contract he got. I've always found that you have to pay more for antiques."
—Joe Sambito, after 36-year-old Joe Niekro signed a lucrative deal with Houston some years ago

Things Overheard at Old-Timer's Gatherings

"Joe, you're the only old-timer whose hair gets thicker as the years go by."
—Joe Garagiola to the rug-wearing Joe Pepitone (whom Jim Bouton described as the "former hairpiece model")

"Our black players are so old they don't even know how to high five."
—Lou Brock, at an old-timer's game

"Ernie Banks is the only player I know who lives in Mister Rogers's Neighborhood."
—Lou Brock, at the same game

"Is it true that you were so depressed during that '69 season that you jumped in front of a bus and it went through your legs?"
—Broadcaster Wally Phillips, to ex–Cub third baseman Ron Santo

"Joe, when they list all the great catchers, you'll be there listening."
—Casey Stengel to Joe Garagiola

Some Final Words About the Role of God in Baseball

"I don't think God gives a damn whether we hit or not. If God cared, Billy Graham would be hitting .400."
—Chris Sabo, Reds third baseman

"Do you think God would mind if you threw your breaking ball over for a strike every now and then?"
—Mets coach Jim Frey, to Baseball Chapel pitcher Pete Falcone

"If God let you hit a home run the last time up, then who struck you out the time before that?"
—Sparky Anderson, to one of his players

"Why is it that Jack Clark can find God but not the cutoff man?"
—Remark made after the outfielder became a born-again Christian

8 The Unavoidable Steinbrenner Chapter

Nobody *wants* to do a Steinbrenner chapter. You go into the book thinking to yourself, "I don't want to do a Steinbrenner chapter. I don't want to give that overbloated bag of bile any more ink than he's already gotten." But then you start doing the research and you see all the psycho things he's done and said and all the people he's made crazy over the years and you say to yourself, "There's no way around it. There's just too much there. I simply can't avoid the guy . . ."

Analyzing George

George is like all the great power-mad tyrants of history. No one can say for sure why he acts the way he does, though a few people have tried to figure it out.

"It's like a dog who has a favorite toy. You know, the way a dog will keep chewing at the toy, tearing at it, kicking it around. I don't mean to compare Mr. Steinbrenner with a dog, but the way he handles this team, well . . . we're the toy."
—Roy Smalley, former Steinbrenner toy

"I don't understand the big deal about George. It's really very simple and very pure. He is first and foremost and forever just a bully. . . . And he fires people in weird ways—he castrates them."
—A "social peer" of Steinbrenner's, as quoted by screenwriter-novelist William Goldman

The one and only George Steinbrenner, here shown trying to swallow his teeth.

"I don't think he's a bad person . . . just a damaged one. This is all Psychology I, understand, but he had a very tough and very rich daddy. And in the dark night of his shredded soul, I believe Steinbrenner wonders, would he have made it had he not been born so rich and privileged? And what rips at him, of course, is this: He'll never know. I know, though. Not a chance."
—William Goldman

George and a Few of His Managers

George's most famous—and most fired—manager was Billy Martin, but there've been many other beleaguered souls who've passed through the Bronx House of Detention (Nelson Doubleday's phrase). How about Stump Merrill? Steinbrenner sized him up this way: "Here we have a fellow who doesn't have a lot of glamour. For the first five years I knew him, I kept calling him 'Lump.' "

Ralph Houk, a link to the great Yankee teams of the early sixties, managed under Steinbrenner in 1973 before leaving for Detroit. The two were not friendly, and George cooked up this conspiratorial idea that Houk's Tigers lay down like lambs at the end of the 1974 season, losing to Baltimore in a year-ending series as a way to keep New York from winning the division. "I know Baltimore won last night," fumed Steinbrenner. "Ralph Houk let them win. Ralph pitched a bunch of young kids so Baltimore would win."

The Führer is not easily pleased. Even when Dick Howser was managing the Yanks to 103 wins and an American League East title in 1980, Steinbrenner criticized him for being outmanaged by Baltimore's Earl Weaver in a game. "Dick Howser is my manager and he's done a helluva job to keep us in first place the way he has. But as a fan, I have a right to question his strategy. . . . You've got to give Earl Weaver all the credit. He's a wizard and our guy's a rookie manager. I wouldn't invite Weaver to Christmas dinner, but you've got to give the devil his due."

In the 1980 playoffs against Kansas City, Willie Randolph was thrown out at home after trying to score from first on a double. The Royals had overthrown the cutoff man, and third-base coach Mike Ferraro thought Willie could make it all the way. But the man who came up with the ball was George Brett, and he gunned Randolph down. Furious at what he saw as an outrageous blunder by Ferraro, Steinbrenner sought out his wife: "Your husband fucked up the game for us!" he screamed in her face.

After Howser came Gene Michael, who was criticized by George for not holding a team practice when George thought he should. Michael tried to be philosophical. "I can live with anything. My mother died in 1978. I went through a divorce. I had friends who died. He can take the job. It won't bother me. I won't resign." George responded, "I'm the boss, I'm the leader, and he should have shown more loyalty. No one anywhere keeps a job acting that way." As usual, The Boss was right, his manager was wrong, and George snapped Stick over his knee in September.

Said Michael, just before the end: "I don't think people know what it's like to work for him. I don't think it's right that I should be constantly threatened by him and yelled at in front of my coaches. He can take the job, but he's not gonna bring me down." But Michael must've been a glutton for punishment because he came back to do George's managerial bidding in 1982 following the firing of the man who replaced *him*, Bob Lemon. But Michael could not please his demanding boss that time either and he was fired again before the season was over.

The Best Question We Ever Heard About What It's Like to Be an Employee of George Steinbrenner

"Seeing as how none of us has ever worked for Genghis Khan, how does it feel to work for George Steinbrenner?"
—Broadcaster Ted Dawson, in an on-the-air interview with Gene Michael

And Though He Wasn't Asked, Don Mattingly Answers the Question

"You come here and you play and you get no respect. They treat you like shit. They belittle your performance and make you look bad in the media. After they give you the money, it doesn't matter. They can do whatever they want. They think money is respect."

George and Yogi

Yogi Berra, one of the mildest of men, got so angry with George that he pelted him with a pack of cigarettes. This was Yogi's response to yet another Steinbrenner tongue-lashing, a familiar if obnoxious rite in which George blamed his manager for whatever was going wrong on the field while conveniently overlooking the fact that *he* was the one who had signed all those horseshit players in the first place. But this time Yogi couldn't take it and lost his cool:

"This isn't my fucking team, it's your fucking team! You make all the decisions. You make all the moves. You get all the players that nobody else wants. You put this team together and then you just sit back and wait for us to lose so you can blame everybody else because you're a fuckin' chicken shit liar!"

Yogi survived this outburst and made it through all of 1984 as Yankee manager, only to be fired 16 games into the next season. When they heard the news his players filed into Berra's office to express their shock and sadness; some were even crying.

Steinbrenner later called this scene "almost humorous," adding, "I could care less what the players think. They're the ones who cost Yogi his job."

Yankee Manager Jokes

"How about that Nolan Ryan pitching a no-hitter? He's been playing for over 20 years. For you Yankee fans, that's over 300 managers ago."
—Jay Leno

"Sooner or later, of course, being the apple of his eye is the same as being the apple of William Tell's eye."
—Dave Anderson, on Stump Merrill being described as the "apple of George Steinbrenner's eye"

"With Billy Martin dead, and with zero population growth an American goal in the 21st century, could George, like a chainsaw–crazy paper mill that fails to recycle, be in danger of running out of managerial timber? How long before Steinbrenner, having exhausted the domestic supply, is forced to hire his first Japanese manager?"
—Alan Greenberg, columnist

Making his triumphant 1990 tour of America, South African activist Nelson Mandela appeared at a Thursday night rally in Yankee Stadium. "You know who I am," Mandela told the cheering thousands as he donned a Yankee cap and jacket. "I am a Yankee!"

Then on Friday, said sports editor Jim Carlisle, George fired him.

The Fight in the Elevator

For the millions upon millions upon millions of Steinbrenner haters around the world, his fight in the elevator following the Yankees' loss to the Dodgers in the 1981 World Series is one of the most gratifying of all memories. The humiliated Steinbrenner, bruised and bandaged, apologizing to New York fans for his team's disgrace. Ah, sweet bird of happiness!

Did the fight really happen the way George said it did? Did he really bust up a couple of young toughs who were mocking him and his beaten team in the hotel elevator? "If the fight really took place the way George says it did," said Orioles owner Edward Bennett Williams, "this is the first time a millionaire has ever hit someone and not been sued."

After that bitter loss—LA came from two down to win four straight—the Doge of New York issued his famous apology to Yankee fans for the way the team played. This did not sit well with the players themselves, particularly Reggie Jackson, who wondered if Steinbrenner was going to apologize if they lost their first spring training game in Fort Lauderdale. George did not like the tone of this remark, and in a snit he let Mr. October walk away from New York. This alone is proof—if any, at this late date, is needed—that George's big mouth has cost him and his team dearly. Reggie walked, and Steinbrenner's Yankees would never again go to the Fall Classic.

Known as a Leader of Men, George Gives an Inspirational Pep Talk to One of His Players

"What the hell were you doing out there? Jesus! You looked like a monkey trying to screw a football out there."
—To an infielder after he made an error

Further Demonstrating His Leadership Abilities, George Assesses a Pair of Younger Pitchers Who Did Not Perform as Well as Expected

"Mike Griffin has fooled us long enough. We found out about him today. You say you can't tell from one outing? The hell you can't. That

does it for him. He won't be pitching for us this year. He has to go back to the minors and work his way up—if he can."
—After Griffin gave up five hits in a five-run inning during a Mets-Yankees spring training game. Griffin was sent down to Columbus the next day and later traded.

"We've given Ken Clay many chances, and he has laid a big fat egg. He doesn't have any heart. If he can't pitch with a 5-0 lead, then he doesn't belong in the majors. Ken Clay has complained about not getting a chance, but he doesn't deserve any more chances. He has let his team down too many times already. He's a morning glory. That's a term we use for a horse who is great in the morning workouts, who looks beautiful but who can't do it in the race. The horse spits the bit, and Ken Clay has spit the bit."
—After Clay, a onetime hot prospect, gave up five runs in the first inning against Kansas City in a September 1979 game; later farmed out and traded.

George Talks Some More About His Players

"If you guys were working for one of my other corporations, you'd all be fired right now."
—Registering his disgust to the team during a losing streak

"He can't play Jack Armstrong of Evansville, Indiana, anymore. He's like all the rest now. He goes into the category of 'modern player with agent' looking for the bucks. Money means everything to him."
—Early in Don Mattingly's career, after the first baseman went to arbitration against George and won a nearly $2-million contract

"Mattingly was being selfish swinging for home runs when he should have been thinking of the team."
—After Mattingly, who had hit eight homers in eight consecutive games in 1987, sprained his wrist on the ninth day of the streak and had to sit out a few days

"The most selfish athlete I've ever known."
—On Dave Winfield, whom Steinbrenner also mocked as "Mr. May" for not helping the club down the stretch

"Baylor's bat will be dead by August."
—After trading Don Baylor to Boston in 1986. (As in so many other things, George was wrong. The classy Baylor helped lead the Red Sox to the American League pennant that year.)

"Righetti and Fisher should have gone home with the vendors."
—After the two Yankee relievers couldn't hold a big late inning lead against Cleveland

"For all the money I'm paying him, your man isn't doing shit."
—To Rich Gossage's agent during 1983 contract negotiations; (a bitter Gossage left after that season).

Answering George

One time before a big game George was addressing his troops in the clubhouse. In an effort to inspire them to greater heights, he told them about the days when he was a top hurdler at Williams College.

"They must've used ankle-high hurdles in those days," cracked Graig Nettles.

That was a good one. Lou Piniella got off another good one the day Steinbrenner was bawling out the team for complaining about having to work out on an off day. "You guys don't know what work is," George had told them. "You're not tough. I know what tough is . . . I've seen it down on the docks where the longshoremen work."

"Aw George," Piniella piped up from the back of the room, "the only time you've been down on the docks was to put gas in your father's yacht."

The honor of "Bluntest Riposte to a Steinbrenner Tirade" belongs, however, to catcher Rick Cerone. After Milwaukee beat the Yankees to even the 1981 divisional playoffs at two games apiece (New York later won the decider), George stormed into the clubhouse and let loose with a furious denunciation of the team that was interrupted by an equally angry Cerone.

"Fuck you, George," he shouted at him. "You never played the game. You don't know what the fuck you're talking about."

Momentarily taken aback, George said, "I pay the bills around here. I'll say whatever I want. And we'll see where you're playing next year."

While not the wittiest insult we've ever heard, Cerone's reply must be given points for bluntness if nothing else, and after George said his piece Rick repeated his: "Fuck you."

George and Graig

Yankee third baseman Graig Nettles used to rib George about lots of things, such as his weight: "It's not hard to stay in good shape really," Nettles said. "The first thing you do is try not to eat four or five desserts a day like he does. He doesn't drink, so obviously he eats a lot to be as fat as he is."

Nettles also had a joke about the much invoked "baseball people" that George supposedly relied on to make his personnel decisions: "They have nine votes, and George has 10," Graig noted.

And then there was the stink that George made after Dave Winfield's book came out, which bore great similarity to Steinbrenner's stinks after Sparky Lyle's and Nettles's books were published: "George isn't big on books, is he? I don't think there's ever going to be a National Library Day at Yankee Stadium."

And so it went. Nettles making his cracks and, as long as he played third like Brooks Robinson, Steinbrenner tolerating them. The two even seemed to have developed an affection for each other after so many years together. But, as so often happened with the Yankee owner, it got a little nasty towards the end, with Steinbrenner trading Nettles on the last day of 1984 spring training and saying how this would be good for the ballclub because Graig had become a bad influence on the younger players.

"He tried to discredit me," said a bitter Nettles. "It's too bad they couldn't just trade me and say good luck. But that's the way the man does things. He deals in character assassination. He's done it before and he'll do it again."

George and Lou

George and Lou Piniella have quarreled many times, first when Lou was a player and later when he became one of Steinbrenner's managerial stooges. Sweet Lou could tattoo a baseball with the best of them, but like the Fat Man himself, he struggled with a weight problem over the years. So George put a clause in his 1982 contract fining Piniella $1,000 for every pound he weighed over 200. Lou sweated and strained, but try as he might he couldn't shed the excess flab. Then, after the media got word (through Steinbrenner, of course) that he had accumulated $8,000 in fines that spring, Lou got mad:

"I am utterly disgusted with George Steinbrenner. All we have ever been told around here is that what happens within the Yankee family is supposed to stay there. It's a sad way for a player to learn that he's been fined—through the press. I'm sick and tired of this . . . To be suddenly treated like Little Orphan Annie is ridiculous."

To which George, who always loved a good, publicity-creating fight, responded: "Sometimes Lou has to be treated like a 19 year old. Everybody in Tampa [Lou's hometown] will tell you that. He knew what he was signing. If I'm a man and my employer was paying me $350,000 a year, which is more than the President of the United States is making, and there are 10 million unemployed people out there earning nothing in this country, I'd sure as hell take seven pounds off to honor my contract. Someday Lou Piniella will be out of baseball and in business. Boy, he'd last five days in business."

But Lou remained one of George's favorites, and after Lou hung up his spikes George appointed him Yankee manager in 1986. The next year they had their notorious "Where is Lou when I want him?" spat, one of the most celebrated of all of George's fights. This occurred in early August when Lou didn't stay in his room like a good little boy to receive a phone call from The Boss. Never mind that Piniella had dutifully sat in his hotel room to hear countless other phone diatribes from George in the past. Like all dictators, Steinbrenner demanded unquestioning obedience at all times. The fact that his call kept ringing and ringing and no one was there to answer it made him batty, and he issued a two-page statement to the press, excerpts of which are recorded below:

"The fact is that Lou Piniella failed to be available to his boss at a preset time on Tuesday afternoon in Cleveland. The simple fact is that Piniella didn't even bother to 'come back for lunch,' if that is where he really was, to get a call from his boss at 2 P.M. He didn't even bother to call me to get word to me that the time was inconvenient for him. I don't know of too many guys—even sportswriters—who if their boss told them to be available at a certain time, wouldn't be there. That type of behavior wouldn't be tolerated by any major newspaper and it won't be tolerated by the Yankees either."

The statement goes on: "The manager says the manager 'doesn't need' to talk to me. A couple of the players think I should not get involved as much as I have. They think they can do better that way, that's just fine. I'll keep the whole month of October open, anxiously awaiting the World Series at Yankee Stadium. They can put up or shut up. Maybe it's about time for it."

Copies of this statement were distributed around the Yankee clubhouse. In a show of support for their popular manager, a few of the players took a match to the statement and burned it in open disregard of Steinbrenner. The advertising slogan for the team that year was: "The Yankees: Where Traditions Are Born." In light of all this, columnist Barry Stanton suggested a change: "The Yankees: Where Traditions are Burned."

Dallas Talks Back

After a long and respected career in baseball, Dallas Green took over as manager of the New York Yankees in 1989. But, as everyone knows, a Yankee manager under Steinbrenner has about as much clout as the guy in the mailroom, and Dallas was fired before the season was over. He did not go quietly, though, and his anti-George statements after his firing are classics of the genre. Said Dallas (to Philadelphia sportswriter Bill Conlin):

"Now George is back with his puppet machine. He doesn't want anybody around that he can't command. He couldn't make me change the lineup. He couldn't make me change personnel. He couldn't make me fine people or do anything I didn't want to do . . . Now he's got the right people back. They'll say 'Yes, George,' to anything he says." And:

"George doesn't know a fucking thing about the game of baseball. That's the bottom line. When you've got a guy who wants total control and he doesn't know my job or the strengths and weaknesses of his ballclub, you've got a big problem." And:

"Let's face it, there is absolutely no hope that their organization will be a winning organization as long as Steinbrenner runs the show . . . It's sad. He has no organization there now. He has absolutely no pride. The ballplayers there now have no feeling of being a Yankee."

After being fired, Green, who had a two-year deal with the Yankees, was offered the managing job of the Cincinnati Reds (later accepted by another House of Steinbrenner graduate, Lou Piniella). But Dallas declined, explaining, "After going through the year I just had with Steinbrenner, I didn't want to jump right back into it again. I'm looking forward to sitting home on my farm in 1991 and collecting George's money."

George and His Staff

George handles his front office people the same way he does his managers and players. He pays them well, but treats them like garbage.

Explaining why his friend Al Rosen resigned as Yankee president in 1979, Bob Lemon echoed a familiar refrain, "You can take just so much shit . . . You got to get out before you choke to death."

Steinbrenner and Rosen argued frequently during Rosen's stint with the club, but, as Graig Nettles has said, "George never listened to him much, anyway. Rosen was just someone to blame when something George did went wrong." So it was with many another employee besides Rosen.

When the Yankees were experiencing a rash of injuries one season, Steinbrenner assessed his strength coach—Jeff Mangold—and his trainer Gene Monahan this way: "Here, I've got a strength coach who can't keep my players from getting hurt, and then I've got this asshole [Monahan] who can't get them healthy again."

The flip side of always blaming somebody when things go wrong is taking the credit when things go well. George is good at that, too. Gabe Paul is credited with dealing for some of the key players—Willie Randolph, Mickey Rivers, Ed Figueroa, Chris Chambliss—that made up the great Yankee teams of the late seventies and early eighties. But Steinbrenner has scoffed at this, turning the credit back to where (in his mind) it belongs: "Paul was in baseball 40 years, 25 as a general manager, and did he ever win a pennant before? You think he made all those moves with this team himself? You think all of a sudden he got so brilliant?"

Syd Thrift is another longtime baseball man who has served in the chaotic Yankee front office. Hired in the spring of 1989 as general manager, he caught flack from George for not cracking down on the outspoken Dallas Green, then engaged in a war of words with the Yankee owner. "It's about time that good ole boy stood up and was counted," said Steinbrenner, and the Virginia-born Thrift resigned after less than a season.

In general, the survival rate of a manager or general manager under Steinbrenner is slightly longer than the life cycle of a mosquito. Though some people such as Clyde King, who served as both manager and general manager with the Yankees, defy the odds and flit about the organization for years. But the banished Dallas Green may have had the best explanation for why King fared so well in the evil kingdom: "Clyde King gets paid a hundred thousand dollars a year for saying yes."

George Among His Peers

Frank Cashen, an executive with the rival Mets, once referred to the Bronx home of the Yankees as "Fort Apache, Yankee Stadium," alluding to the guns-and-blood Paul Newman cop movie. When he read this in the papers George was ready to go to blows: "If Frank Cashen made that comment, it doesn't surprise me, because I've never thought much of Frank Cashen. He's not much of a man to say that. I don't want a remark by a man I have so little respect for to upset my fine relationship with [Mets owners] Nelson Doubleday and Fred Wilpon, but if Mr. Cashen cares to come and discuss the comment with me in a room somewhere. . . ."

Cashen later said he had been speaking off the record, and when questioned by reporters he refused to say whether or not he made the remark. Steinbrenner was unpersuaded: "Frank Cashen wouldn't have the guts to say whether he really said it, but I believe he did."

George also had an intense rivalry in the early '80s with Chicago White Sox co-owners Eddie Einhorn and Jerry Reinsdorf (who's now a friend and ally of his). After the Yankees signed White Sox outfielder Steve Kemp to a big contract, Reinsdorf snapped, "We should consider putting another franchise in New York," and called Steinbrenner irresponsible. George responded by comparing the Einhorn and Reinsdorf pair to both the Katzenjammer Kids and Abbott and Costello.

The antagonists clashed again in a checkbook duel over pitcher Floyd Bannister, and this time the Sox, those lucky stiffs, won out. Reinsdorf crowed, "We beat fat George out of that one!"

Commissioner Bowie Kuhn slapped fines on all of the principals and ordered them to cease and desist.

George During the Years of Collusion

"I know that George Steinbrenner wanted to hire me. I could see it in his face. I could hear it in his voice. He finally had to say, 'Sorry, buddy, I can't do it.' Steinbrenner said no one told him what to do. In fact, he swore on his mother's name about it. All I can say now is, 'Poor Mom.' "

—Jack Morris, the star free agent pitcher who came close to signing with the Yankees in 1985 but who, because of the collusion practiced by Steinbrenner and the other baseball owners, did not.

After a long and nasty argument with the dictatorial Steinbrenner,
Dave Winfield left Yankee hell for the Angels.

George and Howie

First Richard Nixon, then Howard Spira. George Steinbrenner has never associated with the right kinds of people. In 1974, after being convicted for making illegal campaign contributions to the committee to re-elect Tricky Dicky, George was suspended from baseball. Then, in 1990, baseball gave George the boot again after he admitted paying Spira $40,000 to supply him with damaging information on one of his own players, outfielder Dave Winfield. Steinbrenner and Winfield were engaged at the time in an ugly dispute over Winfield's charitable foundation, among other things.

George's payoff scheme backfired when Howie got nasty—he referred to Steinbrenner as "George Von Steinhitler" in a note—and tried to extort money from him. Howie threatened George and his family with violence if he did not cooperate (i.e., give him more money), and Spira has since been convicted for his evil doings and sent up the river where he belongs. Nonetheless, George's actions have been justifiably condemned and ridiculed as well. "They're going to have 'Howie Spira Night' at Yankee Stadium before long," says Mike Lupica. "Show up with lively information about Yankee players, and the owner will give you forty grand."

For his conduct, George was banished from baseball—a punishment he agreed to in writing. But the ink was barely dry before he began saying that Commissioner Fay Vincent had conned him.

"The spirit of the agreement was that it wasn't supposed to be a ban," he said. "But within ten minutes of the time we signed it, Fay Vincent went to his press conference and said, 'It is a permanent suspension.' He also said that I can't even go to a ballgame without his permission. That's a lie! That's a lie!" Vincent replied that it was George who was lying about their agreement, that in fact it was a permanent suspension. He added, "I can't think of anyone other than Saddam Hussein I'd rather have making these complaints."

But Steinbrenner, whose people had been engaged in a behind-the-scenes campaign to discredit the commissioner, could not see the aptness of the Saddam comparison and replied self-righteously, "I'm truly sorry that Fay Vincent would make such a statement, as it only underscores the questions that many people have raised recently about his ability to serve as commissioner and to act rationally."

Act rationally? And he's the guy handing out unmarked 50s and 100s in a suitcase?! Everything about George defies rationality, including this thing with Howie the Mole. No matter what happens, though, New York Yankee fans will always recall with delight and glee that day —July 30, 1990—when the announcement was made that the man who had brought them so much misery was being banned from the game. As *Time* magazine put it, "July 30th may become a patriotic holiday in New York City and wherever the proud traditions of baseball are honored."

Another Person Besides the Commissioner Who Notices the Similarities Between George and Saddam Hussein

"The United Nations has universally denounced Saddam Hussein, the Europeans are calling him the Hitler of the Middle East, and the Arabs are calling him the Butcher of Baghdad. The Americans, though, are calling him the Steinbrenner of Iraq—and you can't get much worse than that."
—Jay Leno, during the buildup to the Gulf War

George's Legacy

"Across nearly five decades, the Yankees epitomized stability. Steinbrenner always loves to talk about that great Yankee tradition, but what he has done is turn this once-great franchise into the laughingstock of baseball."
—Bill Madden, sportswriter

"George's legacy is not the World Series winners of '77 and '78 or having the best record of any team in the '80s. His legacy is these past five seasons—teams with worse and worse records culminating in last year's last place finish. George talked a lot about tradition, but it was all phony. It was just him trying to be part of the tradition. You can't manufacture tradition in a plastic way. You have to have a certain class to go with it."
—Tony Kubek, ex-Yankee shortstop, 1991

The Last Word on George

The day was April 27, 1982. The first time Reggie Jackson returned to Yankee Stadium after being let go by George and signed by the California Angels. Ron Guidry was on the mound for the Yankees, and Reggie tied into one of his offerings for a home run that was as long as it was sweet. After being bad-mouthed by Steinbrenner who considered him old and washed up, Reggie had made his statement.

And now it was the fans' turn. First in small groups, then gathering force quickly around the entire stadium, they delivered their own spontaneous and rhythmic message:

"STEINBRENNER SUCKS! "STEINBRENNER SUCKS! STEINBRENNER SUCKS!"

For all those Yankee fans who suffered so long under George's inglorious reign as owner, it was a marvelous, never-to-be-forgotten moment.

"STEINBRENNER SUCKS! STEINBRENNER SUCKS! STEIN-BRENNER SUCKS!"

Reggie: "The fans made a vocal expression that George made a mistake letting me go. They were able to say something a little more directly than I could."

Indeed.

All the Owners and 9
Front Office People Who
Are Not George
Steinbrenner

s you may have surmised, this chapter is all about the baseball owners and front office people who are *not* George Steinbrenner (and thankful for it, I'll bet). Plus there's some trade talk, some commissioner talk and, for all those gluttons for punishment who are not thoroughly sick of the subject by now, even some money talk. But we keep *that* to a minimum.

Broomhilda of the Reds

Marge Schott once said that George Steinbrenner was "ruining baseball." Boy, talk about the pot calling the kettle black . . . After hearing this remark by Marge, George said that he'd never buy a car from her. A great many baseball fans would like nothing better than to see Marge and George driving together in one of the Buicks she sells, experience a sudden brake failure, and go hurtling off a cliff.

Although Schott has been called "Steinbrenner's long lost sister," she is more reminiscent of Charlie Finley, the rapscallion ex-owner of the Oakland A's. To paraphrase Jim Murray, she knows everything about baseball that a career as a society matron and selling cars has taught her. Like Finley, she is a famous tightwad. While she has brought a world championship to Cincinnati, a Finleyesque sort of turmoil has come along with it. The happiest people in the Reds organization, employees and players alike, are often the ones who just got out. Also like Finley, she has a fondness for animals. Whereas Finley adopted a mule, Charlie O, as the team mascot, she had Schottzie, the fabled bow-wow.

Unlike Finley, though, she's more of a joke than a menace. During the controversy over whether a Japanese-led group should buy the Mariners, one baseball owner cracked, "Besides, would we rather have the Japanese or Marge Schott?" Meaning: Do you want folks with bucks or folks with Buicks? Schott is that rarest of individuals—a female baseball owner—and this may help explain her outcast state. "I know people say, 'Oh her and her stupid dog.' But who else would aggravate baseball men besides me?" she queries. Of course, Marge aggravates both men and women, but that's beside the point.

Marge's best friend was Schottzie the St. Bernard, who succumbed to cancer during the 1991 season. Not everyone was choked up about this. "That damn dog tried to bite me," recalled Mitch Webster. "I was going underneath the stands to hit in the cage one time, and Marge and Schottzie came out of the elevator. I like dogs, so I bent down to pat him and he came after me, snarling and barking. Marge said, 'Stay away. He doesn't like people in uniform.' " That may be why the Reds players generally kept their distance from Schottzie, too.

Marge and Schottzie were closely identified, so much so that Joe Magrane thought some kind of weird symbiosis was going on. "I've heard of the phenomenom of the master taking on the appearance of the dog. But I never knew it went so far as the master taking on the thinking process," he said.

Marge had the big idea during the 1990 World Series of having her players wear "Schottzie caps," those ridiculous Reds caps with floppy dog ears on the sides. Rob Dibble, among many others, rebelled: "She might pay me, but she's not going to make a fool out of me." Don't be so sure of that, Rob. Tony Kornheiser joked that instead of World Series rings Marge was going to give out "gold-plated pooper scoopers."

The joke among her employees in the Reds organization is that they wished she'd treat them like dogs; they'd be better off. Sportswriter Jerry Crasnick says that turnover is high because Schott "pays her employees nothing and compensates [them] with a total lack of appreciation." He adds, "Most are content to keep their mouths shut upon leaving the Reds. The consensus is, why trash the warden after you've been released from prison?"

Tim Sabo, a former financial controller with the Reds, is one inmate who did not keep his lips buttoned. Sabo (no relation to Chris, the third-baseman) filed a lawsuit against his ex-boss in October 1991 charging her with all sorts of underhanded doings. Such as asking him to cook the books for tax reasons, trying to bribe him, and ordering the forging of players' signatures to cash in on frequent flyer vouchers. The foul-mouthed . . . er, blunt-spoken . . . heiress denies everything, and has called Sabo "a little son of a bitch" on television.

Sabo also accused Schott of telling him not to hire black people. "I don't want their kind here," he quotes her as saying. The Reds owner denies this with equal vehemence, and in an interview with a Cincinnati newspaper summed up her views on racial tolerance thusly, "There's nobody who respects black people, good black people, more than I do."

Schott has had public spats with other ex-employees, notably Reds team physician Michael Lawhon, who resigned at the end of 1991. "I cannot continue to compromise my quality sports medicine in light of the present management," Lawhon said, explaining his resignation. He cited the Reds for not giving him adequate medical equipment to work with and constantly second-guessing him. "I cannot and will not continue to engage in a situation that has a front office which does not consider the medical team and its players' health a priority," Lawhon said. Marge said the doctor was all wet and hired somebody else.

The medical issue arose most prominently with Eric Davis, who sat out over one third of the 1991 season because of ankle and other injuries as well as problems related to the lacerated kidney he suffered in the World Series the year before. After being traded to the Dodgers in the off-season, Davis said that the departed Lawhon was right. "The whole thing last year was that I tried to come back too soon with my ankle and didn't get the proper level of care that I deserved. I've seen and talked to more people this morning, doctors and trainers, who expressed an interest in my health, than I did my whole last year at Cincinnati."

Jerry Crasnick says that Davis and Schott were bickering so much in their last year together they resembled Ralph and Alice Kramden of "The Honeymooners." Now that Davis is gone, somebody will have to step forward to play Ralph to Marge's Alice. ("To the moon, Marge, to the moon!") Lou Piniella is an obvious candidate. So is fly-off-the-handle reliever Rob Dibble. Until she unloosened the pursestrings for him, Barry Larkin was making noises about how the Reds were a bunch of pennypinchers and they weren't going to win if they didn't spend some money. One person who won't play the role is Stan Williams, who was canned as Reds pitching coach because Marge wanted him gone. "Broomhilda got me," he explained. "According to what I was told by the manager, the owner was unhappy with the pitching. At first, it was hurtful not to be wanted. But after taking everything into consideration, I might be the lucky one." That's right, Stan. You're out of jail.

Rob on Marge, Marge on Rob

Rob Dibble, on Marge Schott: "If she was a man, other men would've kicked her ass by now."

Marge Schott on Ron Dibble: "Oh, Rob's like a little baby sometimes. I have to smack him. I'll talk to him, smack his arm, and tell him to be quiet."

Q & A with Marge

Baseball fans tend to think that most owners do not know their head from a hole in the ground, to put it nicely. Baseball fans may be right. Witness Marge Schott. She once wanted Cincinnati's scouts fired because, as she said, "all they do is sit around all day and watch ballgames." Here is still more evidence, an actual 1988 interview with Schott conducted by an actual newspaper, the *Cincinnati Post*, four years after she bought the Reds.

Q: "Who do you see as your toughest competitor?"

Schott: "Well, I hope it's St. Louis."

Q: "I mean in the division."

Schott: "Let me see. I don't know. Maybe the Kansas City Royals."

Q: "I mean your division."

Schott: "Well, Pittsburgh's got some young men coming, and Los Angeles is coming back."

Just think. People like Schott—well, nobody is exactly like Marge Schott, but you know what I mean—are signing the checks and making the important decisions on ballclubs in both leagues. Scary.

This Guy Married Jane Fonda?

He founded CNN. *Time* Magazine named him "Man of the Year." He won the America's Cup. He's worth billions *and* he's married to Jane Fonda. But until he brought in the right people and kept his nose out of things, Ted Turner was a complete bust when it comes to owning and operating a major league baseball team. Two assessments of the baseball savvy of Captain Outrageous:

"If you watch the Braves for about two weeks, you will understand perfectly why Ted Turner would think that Casablanca would be a better movie in pastels. The man loves mediocrity. He worships mediocrity. He sends his announcers to mediocrity school, where they listen to tapes of Jay Randolph and Curt Gowdy 16 hours a day. He collects mediocre players and mediocre pitchers and hires mediocre managers to direct them."
—Bill James

"In 1980, Turner signed Claudell Washington for $3.2 million over four years. The news prompted Phillies owner Ruly Carpenter to leave baseball in disgust. The kicker: Turner, at the re-entry draft in New York, negotiated with Washington's agent, but thought it was Dave Winfield. Al Hrabosky, now a Cardinals broadcaster, will get paid by Atlanta through the year 2019. Reliever Rick Camp, through an agent, was set to demand $1.5 million over three years. Turner retorted with a onetime, take-it-or-leave-it offer: $1.9 million over four years. Camp almost sprained an elbow grabbing the pen."
—Mark Whicker

So You Want to Be Baseball Commissioner?

If you do, check out a few of the things that have been said about former commissioner Fay Vincent on: first, the Nintendo Mariners controversy; then, that old standby, The Great DH Debate. You may then want to reconsider.

"To judge by baseball's first reaction, you'd think the Japanese intended to move the Mariners to Tokyo. Or you'd think they wanted geisha girls on the foul lines . . . Good heavens, you'd have thought Godzilla was about to drop Fay Vincent from the Empire State Building."
—Dave Kindred, columnist

"David Duke might have some speeches all typed up and ready to go when Fay has to stand up and defend the White Male Baseball Owners' position. The good ol' boys were exposed for the racists we all knew they were, and now baseball's high court is about to be exposed in a similar manner . . . What would have been Vincent's reaction if Yamauchi, president of Nintendo of Japan, approached him with a new, improved, whiz-bang version of a hand-held video game called Major League Baseball, accompanied by a $20-million check to cover rights fees? That baby would be in the bank before the ink was dry on the signature."

—Bart Wright, columnist

"This [the designated hitter rule, which Vincent opposed] is not something the commissioner needs to waste his time talking about. Each league has its own rule; the American League is not about to change the rule . . . This idea that it decreases the strategy is nonsense—you know, the big double switch. Any imbecile managing a team could do a double switch."

—Jerry Reinsdorf, White Sox chairman

"I don't know if the commissioner of other leagues dictates the rules of the game."

—Pat Gillick, Toronto general manager

"This game isn't being played for the aesthetic enjoyment of the commissioner. Should the game be played the same everywhere? If that's the case, then you're going to have to tear down Fenway and some of these other parks that are unusual. I mean, it's the very nature of our game. The environments are very different in both leagues. The ballparks are different, the surfaces are different. I think the DH is just another element of that."

—Andy MacPhail, Minnesota general manager

Blewie Kuhn

Nobody was picking on Fay in particular. I mean, people *were* picking on Fay, but there's nothing new about people picking on the commissioner of baseball. The late commissioner Happy Chandler had an aide named Muddy Ruel. His job, said Red Smith, was "to keep Happy's foot out of Happy's big mouth." More recently, Howard Cosell intimated that the Pete Rose controversy killed Vincent's predecessor, Bart Giamatti, though this is definitely going too far. Rose can be blamed for lots of things, but murder is not one of them.

Anyhow, for a person with largely a figurehead job who frequently functions as the owners' toady, the baseball commissioner does catch a good amount of flack. For further illustration, we bring you Bowie Kuhn and a sampling of some of the things that were said about him during his term as baseball's grand Poobah.

"Emperor Kuhn should be glad he's an American. If this were Russia, he'd be sent to Siberia and all traces of him expunged."
—Jerry Holtzman, sportswriter

"Dishonest and unethical."
—Reds executive Dick Wagner

"This Johnny Come Lately has done more to destroy baseball in the last six weeks than all of its enemies have done in the past 100 years."
—Houston owner Roy Hofheinz, after Kuhn ruled against him on a 1969 trade; (Hofheinz called him "Blewie Kuhn," as in "he blew it").

"Mr. Kuhn told Willie Mays to get out of baseball. I would like to offer the same advice to Mr. Kuhn."
—Howard Cosell, after the commissioner suspended Mays (and later Mickey Mantle) from baseball for working for a New Jersey casino

"I believe a commissioner should be a dictator. If he's a darn good dictator, you give him a gold watch now and then. If he's a lousy dictator, you fire him. Bowie Kuhn is not a good dictator. Authority only goes to those who have the guts to use it and he doesn't use it. How can he allow the American League to play one kind of baseball with the designated hitter and the National League play another type of baseball?"
—Ray Kroc, the late Padres owner

"Every successful Italo-American is always suspected of having ties to the underworld. The reason that Bowie Kuhn will never approve Mr. De-Bartolo happens to be that Mr. DeBartolo is of Italian descent. It's that simple."
—Vince Bartimo, an Edward DeBartolo employee, after Kuhn blocked the 1980 purchase of the Chicago White Sox by his boss

"Bowie Kuhn was prejudiced and I think that's what kept us out of baseball."
—Edward DeBartolo, Sr.

"I understand that Mr. Kuhn requested that he present me with the award for the outstanding moment of the 1970s. However, looking back on that time, I remember the commissioner did not see the need to attend."
—Henry Aaron, refusing to attend a banquet with Kuhn because Kuhn did not go to Atlanta to see him hit No. 715

"His honor, the idiot in charge."
—Charlie Finley, an old friend, describing Kuhn

Ubie-Doobie-Do

Before Bart and after Bowie came Peter Ueberroth, who rolled back Bowie's suspension of Mantle and Mays and performed the Olympian feat of finally bringing all the baseball owners together. Of course, a judge later called that "collusion," but hey, you can't win 'em all.

"It was supposed that Peter Ueberroth, having ridden into office on a wave of Olympian acclaim, would restore some of the old [Kenesaw Mountain] Landis clout to the office. He had charm, appearance and a track record paved with profits. He quickly won the support of the common man. He gave him a vote on the use of the designated hitter. I'm sure he must've done something else. I haven't been keeping book on it."
—Furman Bisher, sportswriter

"That wasn't a home run Peter Ueberroth hit in his Mantle-Mays decision. It was a double, as in double standard."
—Phil Pepe, criticizing Ueberroth's 1985 decision to reinstate Mickey Mantle and Willie Mays, while ignoring the lesser known Sparky Lyle who also worked for a casino

"Ueberroth's announcement of the reinstatement of Mickey Mantle and Willie Mays was a blatant pandering for public favor."
—Larry Fox, columnist

"One can only step back in honest admiration of what good can be accomplished when two self-promoting schemers see votes at the other end of injustice."
—Columnist Bernie Lincicome, after Ueberroth and Jesse Jackson reacted strongly to Al Campanis's notorious 1987 remarks that blacks lacked "the necessities" to manage

"Peter Ueberroth? Some manager he turned out to be. If he didn't invent collusion, he certainly looked the other way while it was going on in baseball. You can make the case that it was the single greatest ownership fiasco in sports history—the penalties imposed on the owners will probably reach $280 million—and Ueberroth was playing golf."
—Mike Lupica

Nasty Things That Marvin Miller, Former Head of the Players Association, Has Said About People

If one man besides Curt Flood deserves the blame—or credit—for making millionaires out of guys who play baseball for a living, it's Marvin Miller. Now retired, he was a tough-as-nails labor negotiator who led the Players Association through strikes, lockouts, propaganda wars and everything else to get major leaguers all the money they deserve—and much, much more. The owners and the baseball establishment hated Miller the way a capitalist hates Karl Marx and, as this sampling of Miller's comments demonstrates, the feeling was mutual.

"The owners were, and are, intent on making the players eat dirt. The owners are insistent that the players bend down and kiss the shoes of the owners."
—At the time of the 1972 strike

"To paraphrase Voltaire on God, if Bowie Kuhn had never existed, we would have had to invent him."
—On the former commissioner, whom Miller has ridiculed for his "inept performance as a thinker and the owners' designated fall guy"

"Kuhn only wanted to pick my brains and there was scant possibility of reciprocation in that department."
—On gestures the commissioner made to be friendly with him

"Ha, ha, ha, the whole thing is funny. Now he's [Kuhn] a federal judge. That's delusions of grandeur to the nth degree. The fact of the matter is that this Swan Song of Bowie is going to be reversed."
—After Kuhn suspended Steve Howe and three other players for drug use in 1983

"The notion that somehow he [Kuhn] will help matters by taking a swing at people who are already down is about as un-American a decision

as I have seen. If it wasn't tragic to the players involved, the whole thing would be comical."
—More from Miller on those suspensions

"*A petty dictator.*"
—On Braves owner Ted Turner

"*Sandy Alderson has been selling this bill of goods for years. I think the record shows that he doesn't know what he's talking about.*"
—On the A's general manager, after Alderson said that financial pressures were making the teams in smaller markets unable to compete with the bigger ones

"*Pompous, righteous, a dilettante.*"
—On another past commissioner, Bart Giamatti

"*What Vincent told the owners is, 'I'll do whatever you want me to do.' In total charge? Yeah, he's in total charge the way Chamberlain was in total charge of Hitler.*"
—On Fay Vincent, after Vincent said that free agency was ruining baseball

Nasty Things People Have Said About Marvin Miller

"*An old-fashioned, 19th-century trade unionist who hated management generally and the management of baseball specifically.*"
—Bowie Kuhn

"*Miller turned insincerity into an art form. Guided by an ego that was the North Star of his life, he followed it wherever it led.*"
—Bowie Kuhn, who also described Miller as "the prisoner of his own ego"

"*There was about Miller the wariness one would find in an abused animal. It precluded trust and affection. It set up a wall against any kind of close approach. I doubt that St. Francis could have surmounted the barrier.*"
—Bowie Kuhn, once more . . . (Get the feeling these two didn't get along?)

"*A mustachioed four-flusher.*"
—Paul Richards, baseball executive, on Miller

Alvin Dark and his boss, A's owner Charlie O. Finley. "They say Alvin Dark is a religious man," said pitcher Vida Blue, "but he's worshipping the wrong God—Charlie O. Finley."

"Somebody in baseball has no sense of humor. Marvin Miller should have been invited to throw out the first ball on Opening Day. After all, he helped throw out the first 86 games of the season."
—Irv Kupcinet, after the 1972 players' strike

"Nobody drove wedges better than Marvin."
—You guessed it: Bowie Kuhn

What People Thought of Charlie Finley

Like Mr. Potter in "It's A Wonderful Life," most people didn't like Charlie O. Finley, former owner of the Oakland A's. But then again he didn't like them either so I guess that made it even.

"He usually manages to louse up whatever he tries. He just does things without class."
—Bill Veeck, former baseball owner

"A menace to baseball."
—Ken Harrelson

"He treated his players like plantation hands."
—Bowie Kuhn (echoing the words of A's pitcher Vida Blue, who said Finley treated him "like a colored boy")

"The Club Owner Most Likely to Louse Up Any Franchise He Gets his Cotton-Picking Paws on."
—Red Smith's title for Finley

"That big asshole."
—Reggie Jackson, ex-Finley employee

. . . And Why They Thought It

Here is Charlie O. in full rant, unleashing an attack on A's manager Alvin Dark in front of the entire Oakland squad:

"I don't know what the fuck you're in this game for, but I'm in it to win. And if you don't get your fucking ass in gear, you're gonna be gone. We won two straight [championships] without you and we can make it three without you, too. All you got to do is write the fucking names down on the piece of paper and let them play. We got the best goddamn team in baseball, goddamnit, and if you can't win with the talent we got you can't win!"

Nice, eh? Makes George Steinbrenner look like a pussycat. We should also probably add that this diatribe took place after the A's lost on Dark's *first* day as manager in 1974. The Oaklanders went on to make it three in a row with the beleaguered Dark at the helm.

Other Owners We Have Known

"George Bush Junior, the owner of the Texas Rangers and the son of the president . . . waffles more than the cook at the International House of Pancakes."
—Bart Wright, columnist

"The guy lied like he always does. Everybody lies. I lie. Just like he lied about [former Royals manager] John Wathan being here for the whole season. I don't see him here. Do you? I rest my case."
—Bo Jackson on Kansas City owner Ewing Kaufman, after Jackson was released from the Royals despite promises from management that he wouldn't be

"Even George Steinbrenner wouldn't book the Democratic national convention in his home ballpark and put his team on the road for three weeks. Dr. John McMullen, you're outta here."
—Baseball America, arguing for the removal of the Astros owner

"Nobody owns a baseball team because he loves baseball anymore. It's financial suicide. Beginning with 1976, the game has been run by agents turning the Steinbrenners and Turners by their tails, and the rest of the owners have had to hustle in the street to keep their egos satisfied."
—Calvin Griffith, former Twins owner

"There was no resentment when you said you were moving to Minnesota. But when you said you were going to take the team along too, then the lynch mobs began forming."
—Columnist Moe Siegel to Griffith, after Griffith moved the Twins from Washington to Minnesota in 1960.

"Right now I feel that Bob Lurie is deserving of the title, 'The most hated man in San Francisco.' I think everybody, including the baseball

owners, would like to keep the team here, but Lurie has looked to the dollar sign.''
—Retired San Francisco judge Francis McCarty, after Lurie announced in mid-1992 that he was selling the Giants to Tampa Bay.

Rating the GMs

"Thank God he [Terry Pendleton] came to us. The man's meant everything to us, and we can thank [Cardinals general manager] Dal Maxvill for that. If he wasn't so stingy, Terry would still be there. He's more concerned about saving money than he is about fielding a good club. What an idiot.''
—Ron Gant, Braves outfielder

Question: "What do Mike Port and Jimmy Carter have in common?''
Answer: "They both look a lot better when they're gone.''
—Joke about former Angels GM Mike Port (once described by Bruce Jenkins as a man who "runs a heartless organization and wonders why the club has no heart")

"The fact is, Larry Himes can't get along with anybody. You could hardly find anybody in the White Sox organization who wasn't happy when he left. There were an awful lot of general managers who wouldn't talk to Larry Himes because they didn't like him and they didn't like his style. This is a man with a severe personality problem. He's emphasized that over and over with his bitterness. The last thing I want is Larry Himes hanging around Chicago and on our payroll.''
—White Sox co-owner Jerry Reinsdorf, on his former general manager, Larry Himes, after Himes was hired by the crosstown Cubs

"Carl played college baseball in Pennsylvania and got two hits in his first game—one in the leg and one in the arm.''
—Florida Marlins owner H. Wayne Huizenga, on team president Carl Barger

"After four years, there's no indication what kind of team Tom Haller is trying to build. The conclusion is inescapable: He doesn't know himself. He has inherited the Spec Richardson disease of solving one problem by creating another.''
—Glenn Dickey, on two former San Francisco general managers

"Getting rid of their veteran infielders, getting rid of Belcher, then Murray . . . I know one player already asked Fred Claire if he was out of his mind."
—Pitcher Mike Morgan, on the Dodgers general manager and his 1991-92 off-season moves

"He's choking the organization to death on bad contracts. . . . What general manager in his right mind, with the exception of Rosen, would want to make a guy like that a millionaire?"
—Columnist Lowell Cohn, questioning the sanity of Giants general manager Al Rosen after Rosen signed Jose Uribe to a big contract

The Kevin Mitchell Trade

It's an axiom of baseball that nobody ever knows right away about trades—only time will tell who made the best deal. But with Kevin Mitchell and the San Francisco Giants, you're going to need to trot out another cliché about time. The one about how it heals all wounds.

The Giants have long had a tradition of making bad trades that were unpopular with the fans, but the deal that sent the power-hitting Mitchell to Seattle in 1991 sparked a reaction unlike any other in recent San Francisco history. "Did Al Rosen fall off his stationary bike and hit his noggin 10 minutes before the deal?" asked Bay Area columnist Dave Newhouse. "No clear-headed baseball man could make such a deal. In exchange for the onetime National League MVP the Giants got three pitchers named . . . well, let Glenn Dickey tell it: "The pitchers they got are named Billy Nobody, Mike Nobody and Dave Nobody. The Giants already have more than enough pitchers like that." Or, as Newhouse said, the Giants "gave up an expensive bottle of Mumm's for three bottles of cheap wine."

Much of the blame for the trade naturally focused on Giants GM Al Rosen. "It doesn't really matter who calls the shots: Horace Stoneham, Tom Haller, Al Rosen—they're interchangeable in this category," wrote Bruce Jenkins. "Give the Giants a big star to trade, and they'll get something out of Ballplayers Anonymous in return—if they get any players at all." Jenkins added a personal note: "Our sympathy goes out to Rosen, because he can finally relax. He was going to trade Mitchell before Christmas, and he got the job done. He'll be out of the public eye, which is good, because he could sure use a rest."

The fans reacted even more unfavorably than the media, blasting Rosen in the Saturday letters column of the hometown *Sporting Green.* "I hope I can exchange gifts with Al Rosen this Christmas," said one. "I'll give Al three sacks of peanuts and he can give me a Ferrari. Thanks, Al." A Ukiah fan thought that the Giants should have traded Rosen rather than Mitchell. Another irate fan suggested that the general manager had "totally lost track of reality." And finally, this diehard from Santa Rosa: "After almost driving off Highway 101, upon hearing the news of the Kevin Mitchell trade on my car radio, I'm desperately trying to think of something positive about the trade. After hours of thinking, I finally thought of something. At least the Giants won't have to sign Bob Walk."

Not everybody was critical, of course. Lowell Cohn expressed the minority opinion that just getting rid of Mitchell was a plus—Branch Rickey's old "addition by subtraction" theme. "If the Giants got two used fielder's gloves and a rosin bag for Mitchell, that would have been enough," said Cohn, who added that the malingering outfielder with the big home-run bat was "a mountain of negativity, a larger than life obstacle that sat brooding by his locker or could be found killing time in the trainer's room almost daily."

It was widely suspected that many of Mitchell's teammates, not to mention Giants management, regarded him as an open sore. After the trade was made, reliever Jeff Brantley offered his view: "We've got other guys who can do the job. We have Will [Clark] and Matt [Williams] who do the things Kevin does, but they're at the park every day ready to play ball. They're never too tired or hurt to play. Kevin wanted to be pampered. Without the distraction of Kevin, it will make us a better team."

A column by Cohn in the middle of the 1991 season helped expose the resentment bubbling beneath the surface regarding Mitchell. In the column an unnamed Giant charged that Mitchell was a bad influence on the club who got special treatment from manager Roger Craig though he deserved none. Mitchell reacted in anger, lashing out not only at his unnamed accuser but also at those of his teammates who might have been talking trash about him. "They're probably jealous of me. What am I supposed to do, come in here and hug everybody every day? If I'm out there doing my job, what else do they want from me?" He added, "I'm not going to worry about it. They're here to play the game, not pop off with their mouth. I never pointed a finger at anyone in my life, so why should they do that to me? If they were any kind of a man, they'd come and talk to me. But I think they're scared of me."

Roger Craig also fumed and fussed about the column and the manhood of the Anonymous Giant. But in light of the comments made by Al Rosen after Mitchell was no longer a part of the team, this may have been partly histrionics. Craig wanted Mitchell out just as bad as Jeff Brantley or Will Clark or anybody.

San Francisco made no secret of its desire to peddle Mitchell at the winter meetings in Miami—a desire that was nearly thwarted when a San Diego woman accused the leftfielder of raping her. But the woman decided not to press charges, freeing the Giants—"Quick, get me the phone!"—to move their big-muscled problem child.

Nevertheless, the club was caught off guard by the nearly universal negative reaction to the trade (from Giant fans), forcing the man who engineered the deal to engage in some damage control. "Roger and I had built up this aura about Mitchell, this tough, hard-playing guy," Al Rosen told Bruce Jenkins in an interview a week after the trade. "Well, it's just the contrary, absolutely a 180-degree difference. It had reached the point where we had to stroke this guy just to get him in the lineup."

Rosen told about an incident in Los Angeles when Mitchell was seen "stone-drunk" at two in the morning, then tried to beg off from playing the next afternoon because of a headache. This was typical, said Rosen. "I just couldn't help but think of the effort on the other guys. Headaches, stomachaches—it's always something with this guy. I mean, come on. We're paying him more than $3 million, telling everybody what a big, tough guy he is, and this is what happens? The situation only got worse, too."

Moving swiftly from damage control into a mild form of character assassination, Rosen explained how he thought the deal would help Seattle: "They've got [Ken] Griffey and [Jay] Buhner and some pitching; they need a righthanded hitter. So it's perfect for them. We don't know what Mitchell could do elsewhere. But based on the evidence we have, and the fact that he's getting older and fatter, he won't do it at Candlestick.

"He reminds me of Richie Allen, in a way, or Bobby Bonds," Rosen went on. "There are certain guys who just aren't cornerstone players to a franchise. They move around constantly, usually getting traded for players with less ability. Seattle is the fourth club that's had Mitchell, and I'm sure he'll see more before his career is over."

Rosen also went out of his way to protect Giants star Will Clark, who was once accused of being a racist by Jeffrey Leonard. "Will doesn't want to get involved, and I don't think he should. If he throws out accolades to Mitchell, everybody will know it's a lie. It's obvious how Will feels about Mitchell, and if you're thinking it's a racial thing, it's really not. Will's a player, and Kevin isn't. That's what it's about."

As for Mitchell's reaction, he was a veritable model of self-restraint compared to his ex–general manager. "He's not going to hurt me," said Mitchell about Rosen. "Whatever he says or however he tries to put me down, it's not going to hurt my feelings. Not at all." But what about this loafing charge, Kevin? "He never had to beg me to play. Never." Mitchell did, however, accuse the Giants of lying to him—saying they told him he wouldn't be traded when, in fact, they were just about ready to advertise him on the Shopping Channel if they couldn't find a buyer for him at the winter meetings. Nor did Mitchell like all the attacks on his character after leaving the Giants. "That's what I don't appreciate. People go by what they hear. They didn't grow up in my neighborhood; they always lived with silver spoons in their mouth. This troublemaker got more heart than all of them do." And if he truly does, the last word about the trade will be his.

More About the Team That Traded Away Orlando Cepeda, Gaylord Perry, Bill Madlock and Others

"Over the years the Giants have been blessed with a string of general managers who couldn't break even on 'Let's Make a Deal.' "
—Bill James

"Every time the Giants trade a starter like Dan Gladden, they get three minor league pitchers named Juan."
—Dave Newhouse

"Whenever the Giants call to talk about trades, I bet more than one general manager has had to hold a pillow over his face to keep from laughing into the phone."
—Lowell Cohn

"When I heard that Zachary Taylor's body was being exhumed, I thought the Giants were looking for another pitcher."
—Bob Sweet, as told to Glenn Dickey

After hearing that Von Hayes had been traded from the Phillies, Lenny Dykstra said, "Great trade. Who'd we get?"

Other Signings, Other Trades: Some Reactions

"Just what I need—another hemorrhoid."
—Yankees manager Bob Lemon, upon learning that Doyle Alexander had signed with the team

"I don't mean to be rude, but who the hell is Johnnie LeMaster?"
—Cleveland second-baseman Tony Bernazard, on learning that the Indians had traded for LeMaster to be their shortstop

"The Cubs traded a horse and they came away with two ponies."
—Frank Robinson, after Chicago traded ace reliever Lee Smith to the Red Sox for Calvin Schiraldi and Al Nipper

"If this had been a prison break, there would have been 24 guys behind me."
—Rick Bosetti, after being traded from a bad Blue Jays team

"This gives me a chance to sign with a contending team. It's kind of like getting out of prison."
—Ken Oberkfell, after being let go by the similarly bad Astros

"You mean I got traded for Dooley Womack? The Dooley Womack?"
—Jim Bouton, after being traded to the Astros in 1969

"The worst part of the trade is that we don't get to face Lilliquist anymore."
—A Padres hitter, after San Diego acquired pitcher Derek Lilliquist from the Braves

"That's too bad. They're the only team I can beat."
—Pitcher Dave Cole, after being told that he'd been sold to the Phillies in the fifties

Gabe Paul Jokes

Gabe Paul was a longtime baseball man who has worked, among other things, as general manager of the Cleveland Indians and New York Yankees. Nevertheless, Bill James is not too impressed with Paul's baseball know-how, and he once made up some jokes speculating on what he'd do if Paul went into other fields of business:

"If Gabe Paul was running a hospital, I'd invest in a mortuary."

"If I was on a ship and Gabe Paul was the captain, I'd try to make friends with a shark."

"If Gabe Paul was an investment counselor, I'd open up a pawn shop."

"If Gabe Paul was selling furnaces, I'd sell smoke detectors."

Passing Thoughts on the Sale of the Seattle Mariners to a Japanese-backed Partnership

Peter Schmuck, the sportswriter, gave his top ten reasons why the Nintendo Corporation should buy the Seattle Mariners. A few of them were: "Japanese owners would be forced to pay millions to lazy, unproductive American players. The Kingdome could be renamed Super Mariner World. New uniforms—blue overalls with red shirt and hat —would revolutionize baseball fashion. And the team would remain in Seattle, which would be a tremendous relief to several other major cities."

Our opinion on the matter is basically the same as Jay Leno's. "I don't mind if the Japanese buy the Mariners," said Leno, "just as long as they don't let Yoko Ono sing the national anthem at their games."

Those Greedy Owners

"Baseball has prostituted itself. Pretty soon we'll be starting games at midnight so the people in outer space can watch on prime-time television. We're making a mistake by always going for more money."

—Ray Kroc, former Padres owner

"Greed stops the owners from really going after the drug problem in the game. They still want to win, and they will overlook a player's drug problems if they think it will help them win . . . There is a lot more to the problem than the public knows. Baseball has covered it up."

—Ken Moffett, former president of the players' association, early 1980s

"The public understands that this baseball strike brands owners with the same stamp so long borne by players—money-grubbing fascists who would climb sequoias to shout lies."

—Sportswriter Edwin Pope, prior to the 1981 strike

"Wasn't the Black Sox scandal of 1919 a case of players taking money for playing not to win? This scandal [the 1985-1987 collusion by owners] was not about just eight men on one club over an eight-game series; it involved all the owners, all the general managers, all the club officials, both league presidents, and two baseball commissioners—over three seasons . . . It was undeniably an agreement not to field the best team possible, tantamount to fixing, not just games, but entire pennant races, including post-season series."

—Marvin Miller, former head of the Major League Players Association

"Nobody gives more pious lip service to the free enterprise system than the typical owner of a baseball club. But he does not want it operating in baseball. In spite of a whole series of court rulings, he still believes his players are property."

—Red Smith

"What they are saying is that you are a chattel of Major League Baseball. You are mine. I own you for five years."

—Player agent Scott Boras, protesting the tougher drafting rules for young players instituted by the owners in 1992

Those Greedy Players

"I've said for years that we're headed for Armageddon. But now we're past the gates. To the Four Horsemen of the Apocalypse—Famine, Pestilence, Death and War—we have added a fifth: Unmitigated Greed. It's going to do us all in. I can't see baseball surviving this."

—Giants General Manager Al Rosen, after Ryne Sandberg signed his $7 million-a-year deal in 1992

"Ballplayers used to come home during the winter and punch a time card or a cash register. They were appreciative of their talent and their opportunities . . . Now they're greedy and obsessed with their own importance. Now they spend the winters in the Caribbean or Hawaii or in a state of anger, going to the first tee while their agents go to another negotiating session to get a salary that still will prove unsatisfying."

—Art Spander, columnist

"Money is probably the main reason. It's out of hand. How are you going to tell a guy making $3 million in his fourth or fifth year to

shut up and listen? The only thing young guys respect in the game is the dollar."
—A's pitcher Dave Stewart, on why younger players don't respect the older veterans the way they used to

"Maybe I ought to do what Jose [Canseco] did, call the organization racist. They sure bent over and kissed his behind, and you can print that. I don't want to talk to [A's GM Sandy Alderson]. I don't want to see him, and I want him to stay out of my way."
—Dave Stewart, angry over not being offered a new contract by the A's before the 1992 season

"Kevin Maas, meanwhile, needs a thinking cap. He hit .220 last year, and the Yankees only raised his annual income from $250,000 to $255,000. 'Is that fair?' says Maas. Actually, it's not, Kevin. You should've taken a pay cut, you pop-up making, strikeout-compiling, double play–hitting pooch of a player!"
—Norman Chad, columnist

"The players don't need all that money. After they get the Range Rover and a spittoon in every room, what do they need it for?"
—Lowell Cohn, columnist

"It's going to be a fun league. We won't have any prima donnas making millions and millions of dollars."
—Dick Williams, former major league manager, taking over a seniors pro team in Florida

"Millionaires masquerading as proletariat, the Limousine Laborers."
—Dick Young, the late management shill, on today's ballplayers

"Enough already. Baseball's winter-long dollar dance, this daily conga line with players shimmying along to the frenzied beat of soaring salaries, has become tiresome. Isn't everyone, with the exception of the wealthy beneficiaries, weary of hearing about the obscene contract totals? . . . The contracts given out in recent months are so out of sync with real-world economics, especially in a recession, that they transcend outrageousness. Indeed, there's something wrong with a society in which a baseball player can earn millions while teachers and police, whose jobs are a zillion times more vital, must scrape along."
—Moss Klein, sportswriter, 1992

Absolutely the Last Damn Thing That Needs to Be Said About Ballplayers and All the Ridiculous Money They're Making These Days

"In the past the owners had the players by the short hairs. Now it's the other way around."

—Bob Grim, commentator

God Bless the Media!

God bless the media! Where would this book be without them? For not only do ballplayers, managers and owners insult one another freely, but the media are in there, too. Print reporters, broadcasters, television people—they're all part of the mix, giving and getting insults with the best of them.

David Cone, Journalist

Every so often, usually around playoff or World Series time, a sports page editor is seized by a paroxysm of the brain and thinks to himself, "Perhaps we should hire one of our local boys to write us a column, thereby giving the devoted readers of this fish wrap an insider's view of the dramatic and possibly historic events that are sure to unfold." Since the column is written by a beat reporter for the paper, sometimes using the taped remarks of the local hero and sometimes not, this "insider's" report is generally a disappointment, tending to resemble the warmed-over mush being served elsewhere in the sporting pages.

But not always. As in the case of David Cone during the 1988 National League playoffs, sometimes the player does actually produce some worthwhile reading. Cone, a pitcher for the Mets, combined with Bob Klapisch of the *New York Daily News* to produce a column worthy of journalistic hit-men everywhere when he blasted the Dodgers following Game 1 of the Series. New York beat Los Angeles, 3–2, coming back to score three runs in the bottom of the ninth after being shut out for eight innings by Dodger ace Orel Hershisher. But Cone was dismissive of Hershisher's effort:

"Hershisher was lucky . . . Doc [Gooden] pitched a much better game. Trouble was, Orel was lucky for eight innings."

Then, in the ninth, Orel's luck ran out and the Mets chased him with a run-scoring double by Darryl Strawberry. This brought Jay Howell in from the bullpen, and Cone rejoiced:

"As soon as we got Orel out of the game we knew we'd beat the Dodgers. We knew even after Jay Howell struck out Hojo. We saw Howell throw curveball after curveball and we were thinking, 'This is the Dodgers' idea of a stopper?' Our idea is Randy Myers, a guy who blows you away with his heat. Seeing Howell and his curveball reminded us of a high school pitcher."

After striking out Howard Johnson, Howell gave up a two-out double to Gary Carter that scored two runs and won the game for the Mets. But when Cone's journalistic offering appeared in the paper the next day, the Dodgers retaliated. They knocked the Game 2 pitcher out of the box in the second inning—a fellow by the name of David Cone—and routed the Mets to even the series. One Dodger joked that Cone had to leave the game so quickly because he had to make an early deadline.

Cone redeemed himself by winning Game 6 for the Mets, and he continued to write his columns for the entire series (a series won by the overachieving Dodgers). But after his controversial debut his columns seemed to lack the same punch as before and they attracted considerably less attention.

How a Misquote, While Not Having One Whit to Do With Why the Underrated Dodgers Beat the Overrated A's, Changed Don Baylor's World Series

The 1988 World Series produced another example of how those slippery little devils in the media can influence the games. In the playoffs against the Mets, LA's Jay Howell was suspended two games for being caught with his glove greased up with pine tar. (Scott Ostler: "Jay Howell is the only pitcher I know who was taught to throw a curveball by Lester Hayes.") But the Dodgers survived his absence to whip the Mets and go on to face the A's in the World Series, where right away Don Baylor started lobbing cherry bombs in the beleaguered reliever's direction.

"What's Howell ever done?" Baylor said before the first pitch was thrown. "He couldn't save games over here [in Oakland], so they got rid of him. We want him in the game, all right."

Referring to Howell's suspension, Baylor went on, "He was right where he wanted to be in Games 4 and 5 in New York. He didn't want to be pitching with all the people screaming at him. He can't handle that. He couldn't handle it when he was in New York with the Yankees. I know. I played with him."

Baylor and Howell had played together a few years earlier. Baylor, in fact, had played with everybody and done just about everything in his long, championship-filled career, so nobody could figure out why he'd say those things. Howell in particular was puzzled: "It looks to me that while doing the forearm bash, one of those A's caught Baylor in the head."

Ah, but when there are problems afoot, a lot of baseball people will tell you: Suspect the media. In this case, at least, they were right. It seems that after the A's swept the Red Sox in the playoffs someone asked Baylor which of the National League teams he'd rather face. He said the Mets. "They had the best record; we're the best two teams. Let's settle it," said Don. And Jay Howell had responded: "We proved we're the best team in the league. Guess we'll have to apologize to Don Baylor now."

But! A reporter passed Howell's remark back to Baylor this way: "Don Baylor should apologize for being in the World Series. He's lucky to be here." Some difference. And it caused the A's DH to mount his verbal counterattack.

Postscript: While making good copy for the hundreds of bored and listless media people with nothing but time on their hands until the games got under way, Baylor's statements did not sit so well with Tony LaRussa, however. The A's manager benched him for virtually the entire five-game Series.

Ballplayers and the Press: A Look Back

It is not true that the current animosity between ballplayers and the press began in 1988 when a beat reporter for the *Boston Globe* walked up to Wade Boggs in the Red Sox locker room and said, "Hey, Wade, what's all this I hear about this Margo chick?" No, in fact, baseball players and the knights of the keyboard have not been real keen on one another for the past 100 years or so.

As proof, we refer you to a document unearthed by Bill Weiss. It is a July 5, 1900, writeup of a game between the minor league Pueblo Hulenites and the Denver Cubs by an anonymous *Denver Times* sportswriter. The hometown Cubs lost, and the writer was not amused:

"The Hulenites snagged a game yesterday and boosted their average, but it was not their fault they did it. Denver went in with the full determination to lose, and there is not a shadow of a doubt that Reilly deliberately and intentionally threw the game and if his rank playing was not intentional he should be given his release immediately, for such perfectly rotten playing as he put up yesterday has not been seen here."

As Bill Weiss points out, the villainous Reilly was batting close to .300 at the time and the Denver Cubs were in first place on their way to the Western League championship. But that did nothing to placate the man from the *Times:*

"Kane was in the box for the Cubs and pitched a miserable game, the men from the South hitting him at will and scoring in all but two of the ten innings. But even at that the game should have been won. To a rooter in the stand it looked as though the men on the team were sore because Kane was pitching and had previously arranged to throw the game. He was given absolutely no support. Sullivan dropped more than he held behind the bat and tried to throw as many as possible away when he threw to second.

"Reilly is king. He so completely queered himself with the crowd in the farce of yesterday that he will never be forgiven if he plays in Denver 100 years. He cannot bat righthanded, which is the way he always tries; nevertheless in the ninth inning yesterday he tried to hit the ball from the left side of the plate, and struck out.

"The rooters were thoroughly disgusted with him and he got the best roasting that a has-been ever did get. It is a good thing the Cubs are going away on a vacation, for such games as yesterday's would soon drop the attendance as the men who love the game will not go out to see such rot as was exhibited yesterday."

Patrick Reusse's Philosophy, and Mine as Well

Frequently the writers who do hit pieces on ballplayers are called out by the players themselves or their supporters. This happened a few years ago to Patrick Reusse, the Minneapolis columnist, after he named Cal Ripken, Jr.—prematurely, it is true—to his "All Washed-Up Team." Jim Palmer, the famous broadcaster and underwear model, thought this was way off base and said a whole bunch of nasty things on the air about Reusse, such as: "He's not even honest. He weighs 50 pounds more than his picture in the paper."

Reusse was not flustered at all. Speaking for journalistic insult artists everywhere, he said, "Palmer's got the same right to take cheap shots at me as I do at ballplayers."

Boswell and the Angels

People have the wrong idea about insults. They think they're mean, spiteful, malicious, negative. But, in fact, sometimes a well-aimed brickbat can be a good thing, a force for positive change. Thomas Boswell, the esteemed *Washington Post* sportswriter, demonstrated this after watching a California Angels team of recent vintage. Appalled by what he saw taking place on the field, he fired up the word processor and started dishing:

"If one big league team makes the blood boil, it's the California Angels. They ought to give their fans a rebate. They're the Me Generation nine. The next time an Angel cheers for a teammate, they ought to stop the game and give him the ball. This club thinks hustle and morale require inoculation."

This was late in the 1984 season. The Angels were supposedly contending for a division title, though you'd never have known it by the way they were playing. "Five days ago, the Angels looked ready for the playoffs," Boswell wrote after seeing them lose to the Royals. "Luckily, they lost five in a row. Now they can go where they really want to be: the beach. Who wants to risk playing in the World Series in chilly Chicago when you know the surf's up at Zuma?"

Boswell added that the Angels faced a "team crisis" against Kansas City. "They were about to win a must-win game—something they've never done. Hey, who wants to ruin a perfect record?"

Now it hardly needs to be said that Boswell is no hack. His articles for the *Post* have been collected into best-selling books and a Pulitzer Prize is probably in his future. But something about this apathetic and lardheaded Angels club—which featured, by the way, names such as Reggie Jackson, Rod Carew, Fred Lynn, Tommy John and Bobby Grich—got stuck in his craw, and he had to spit it out. "Take the money and walk" was the team's motto, Boswell said.

"The Angels have no past, no present and no future," he concluded. "They arrive at the park on time, make sure their uniforms fit nicely, give a passable effort and make sure they get the best table at the best restaurant in the town after a game. It's a heavenly life for them. But it's hell to watch."

After the piece came out—if John Simon was a baseball fan, he could not have done it better—Angels owner Gene Autry and president Buzzy Bavasi both called Boswell to thank him for saying what he did. Bavasi said he only wished Boswell had written it a month earlier because it might've shaken the team up and embarrassed them into playing better.

Then, on the last day of the season, someone posted copies of the article around the California clubhouse. And how did the players react when they saw this tastefully worded assault on their abilities and professionalism? Mike Witt strode out to the mound for the Angels and pitched a perfect game.

As Casey used to say, you could look it up.

Talkative Tim

Tim McCarver has gone from being Steve Carleton's personal battery mate to exchanging chit-chat with Paula Zahn in a ski chalet in the French Alps at the 1992 Winter Olympics. Now *that's* progress. Although it's safe to say he'll never be a Jim McKay ("I knew Jim McKay. You're no Jim McKay . . ."), he is still a vast improvement over Brent Musburger. But that may be damning with the faintest of praise. . . .

Anyhow, if people have a beef with McCarver (and some do) it's that he's a mite too . . . *analytical.* And he won't stop talking. Jack Buck, his former broadcast partner on CBS, says that sometimes a director has to tell an overly gabby announcer, "Shut the fuck up!" You get the feeling that directors have had to offer similar commands to McCarver. Some more opinions of Talkative Tim:

> *"Tim McCarver is as opinionated as any five unemployed inhabitants of Wrigley Field."*
> —Phil Mushnick, sportswriter

> *"I guess we should be thankful McCarver was not aboard the space shuttle Discovery, where he would have taken several light-years to explain zero gravity."*
> —Columnist Norman Chad (who said that McCarver's voice sounded "like Half and Half that's gone sour")

> *"Bring back live people who sound like human beings and not encyclopedias. Your voice is as interesting and as alive as the Sahara Desert. You are a Monday morning quarterback wimp, a marshmallow mouth."*
> —An unidentified fan writing to McCarver

"This babbling fool repeated himself, stating the obvious ad nauseum, missing important plays and generally making a damned nuisance of himself. CBS ought to be drawn and quartered for besmirching such a wonderful experience."
—A disgruntled viewer after McCarver's performance on the 1991 World Series on CBS

"The guy constantly explains things that don't need explaining, and spends so much time trying our patience with his stabs at being clever that of course now and then he's going to tell you something you don't know."
—Steve Kettmann, columnist

"My English is better than McCarver's arm ever was."
—An upset Manny Trillo, after McCarver made a joke about the Venezuelan-born infielder's English

Random Observations of Some of Our Friends in Broadcasting

"Harry Caray has a large following, which means American must like senile gents. When was the last time he said something insightful? 1979? Holy Cow!"
—*Baseball America*, on the Cubs announcer

"You have to be in the mood for Harry Caray. If you're in a bad mood, his open pompon waving on WGN and slobbering will only make things worse."
—Sportswriter Jim Van Vliet (who also commented that Caray's partner in the booth, Steve Stone, has a voice that "sounds like he has a clothespin on his nose")

"Bad for baseball: The Numbers Man, Steve Physioc. If he were banned from using statistics in his broadcasts, he would have absolutely nothing to say."
—Tim Keown, on the ESPN announcer

"Like Fred Flintstone on amphetamines."
—Norman Chad, describing the announcing style of another member of the ESPN stable, Chris Berman

"ESPN employs a bunch of yo-hos doing bad Vin Scully imitations. What kind of world is this when Ron Fairly is the standard of competence?"
—Gary Peterson, columnist

"Monte Moore seems like a nice man, but he assaults you with his raging homerism. When the A's and White Sox rumbled in Chicago, you half-expected to see him on the field looking to put a headlock on Bobby Thigpen."
—Gary Peterson

"I heard the doctors revived a man after being dead for four and a half minutes. When they asked what it was like being dead, he said it was like listening to New York Yankees announcer Phil Rizzuto during a rain delay."
—David Letterman

"On the Mt. Rushmore of baseball announcers, there are only four faces: Red Barber, Mel Allen, Vin Scully and Ernie Harwell . . . And right now, there's some defacing going on atop the mountain. A balding, bulging man in a Michigan sweatshirt is chiseling away at Harwell's features. This mean-spirited individual, whose alias is 'The Pasadena Pushover,' plans to have Harwell faceless by October. It will never work. You can fire a legend, but you can't deface him. Bo Schembechler, whose background is college football and foul moods, is trying to do both anyhow."
—Dave Newhouse, prior to the much criticized 1991 ouster of Harwell as Tiger broadcaster by Schembechler and others in the Detroit front office

"First of all, he's stupid. He overbid for baseball by close to a half-billion dollars, then after investing in the NBA all those years, he gives it up just when it's on the cutting edge of turning a profit. Those two moves will go down in broadcasting history as the dumbest ever."
—Brent Musburger, on CBS Sports President Neal Pilson; (Musburger was fired as a broadcaster by CBS).

Question: *"What are the most frightening words imaginable?"*
Answer: *"You are looking live at Fenway Park, and I'm Brent Musburger."*
—Joke told by Red Sox fans, when it appeared that Musburger might be broadcasting baseball

Part of a ballplayer's job is to cooperate with the media, even if they look goofy doing it. Here, Gary Carter proves the point.

"He talks very well for a guy who's had two fingers in his mouth all his life."
—Gene Mauch, on pitcher-turned-broadcaster Don Drysdale

"Reggie Jackson was a better rightfielder than a TV analyst—and probably still is. He tells a great story in person, but on the air he spews clichés nonstop, and is the ultimate apologist on behalf of the players."
—Gary Peterson

"Joe Morgan is becoming a parody of himself. Morgan is intelligent, but he's often condescending and sometimes he tries to make us believe routine baseball decisions are some form of rocket science."
—The Sporting News

"I looked up the definition of a star. It said it's a self-contained mass of gas. I'm not arguing."
—Pat Brickhouse, describing her husband, Cubs broadcaster Jack Brickhouse, at a roast in his honor

"At any given time at the Globe, *half the staff is on deadline and the other half is in makeup."*
—Norman Chad, on the proliferation of sportswriters-turned-broadcasters at the *Boston Globe*

"Men without intellect, without training, without my background at law, and without the spontaneity of articulation that I possess."
—Howard Cosell, on athletes-turned-broadcasters (a species he derided as "jockocracy")

"When the action is at its peak, you should shut up and let the scene tell the story. But some people, like Cosell, feel a need to be a part of the moment and can't stay quiet. Jerkocracy, if you will."
—Tony Kubek

More Broadcasting Notes: The Former Commissioner of Baseball Talks About the Game's Special Relationship With Cable Television

"Where would ESPN be without baseball? There are only so many billiards matches and tractor pulls that you can televise."
—Fay Vincent

Lines That Joe Garagiola Has Heard in Derogatory Reference to His Bald Head

"Hey, Joe, is that sun roof standard equipment on that body?" (From Bill Madlock)

"Put a hat on, Joe. The glare is killing me." (This line, and the next half-dozen, are from acquaintances.)

"You must've had wavy hair because it waved goodbye."

"Joe, did you get a crew cut? Because if you did, I think the crew bailed out."

"I think you better get a bigger bed, Joe. You must be rubbing up against the bedpost."

"Joe, you know what stops falling hair? The floor."

"You must have to pay double for your haircut—half to find it and the other half to cut it."

"Joe Garagiola is an inspiration to young athletes everywhere. I've never seen this man with a drink, a cigarette or a comb." (Dean Martin)

And Joe's Revenge When Somebody Gives Him a Bald Set-up Line That He Can Knock Out of the Park

Joe hears these lines all the time. Or so he says. People who think they're being funny making some crack about the fact that he's a skinhead. In a certain mood Joe might laugh along with them and repeat the Allan Simpson line about how his head is actually "a solar panel for a sex machine."

Then there was the time some guy came up to him and, rubbing the top of Joe's head, said, "That feels just like my wife's bottom."

Now this one Joe could handle. This one Joe hit out of the park. "You know, you're right," he said with a lewd grin, "it *does* feel like her bottom."

Choice Bits from Bob Uecker's Comedy Routine

Most insult humor is directed at somebody. But Bob Uecker (aka Mr. Baseball, the man in the cheap seats, the Lite Beer commercial guy, the sitcom star, Johnny Carson's pal, and a broadcaster for the Milwaukee Brewers during the season) has carved out a nice little niche by directing his insults at himself and his less than illustrious playing career. A few choice samples:

"I remember my frustrating days as a catcher in Philadelphia. The general manager told me they had a very young pitching staff and asked me to help the best way I could. He asked me to quit."

"With Philadelphia, I'd be sitting on the bench and Manager Gene Mauch would say, 'Grab a bat, Bob, and stop this rally!' Or he'd send me up to bat and tell me to go for a walk."

"I was such a bad hitter that Gene nailed my bats to the rack so I couldn't get them out. I led the league in homers, RBIs and lies."

"I set records that will never be equaled. In fact, I hope 90 percent of them don't even get printed."

"When I looked to the third base coach for a sign, he turned his back on me. I was offered a job as a coach—a second base coach."

"When I played, they didn't use fancy words like [emotional distress]. They just said I couldn't hit."

"Anybody can play sober—I liked to get out there and play liquored up."

"They said I was such a great prospect that they were sending me to a winter league to sharpen up. When I stepped off the plane, I was in Greenland."

"In 1962 I was voted Minor League Player of the Year. Unfortunately, that was my second year in the majors."

"Not .201 or .199. A cool .200. A lot of retired players joke about being a career .200 hitter, but I was the genuine article."

"The highlights of my career? I had two: the day I got an intentional walk from Sandy Koufax, and when I got out of a rundown against the Mets."

"My greatest thrill in baseball was the day I saw a fan fall out of the upper deck in Philadelphia's Connie Mack Stadium. When he got up and walked away, the crowd booed."

"I found out my career was over in a strange way. I was with the Braves and I was getting dressed for a game and a coach came over and told me that visitors weren't allowed in the clubhouse."

"I still miss not playing. I miss the small events, like coming into the clubhouse after a big game and having your teammates pounding on your back, jumping on you, trying everything to keep you out of the next game."

"If I was playing today, I'd be a million-dollar player. Is that scary or what?"

Ron Luciano and Earl Weaver

Ron Luciano is a former major league umpire-turned-media personality who, like Bob Uecker and Joe Garagiola, makes a nice living telling humorous stories at his own expense. And he does have a lively wit. For example, Luciano's description of beefy umpire Ken Kaiser, who used to wrestle professionally: "His body looks like a barrel on which two arms had been stuck backward. His face? Promoters made him wrestle with a mask on." Besides himself and his fellow umpires, a valuable source of comedy material for Luciano is Earl Weaver, the Hall of Fame–bound manager of the Baltimore Orioles who used to be his chief foil. Though both have been out of baseball for years, Luciano still makes cracks about the pint-sized Weaver whenever he can:

- "There are two things that every umpire on the field thoroughly dislikes (two and a half, counting Weaver)."
- "When I started umpiring school I didn't even know what an indicator was. It looked more like a little plastic toy than anything else. I figured anything that small had to be easy to handle and fun to play with. Later in my career I made the same mistake about Earl Weaver."
- "I tried not to eject anyone unless they forced me to throw them out. Except Earl Weaver, of course, but that was just recreation."

- "A lot of young umpires' first ejection was Earl Weaver, as well as their second, and their third . . ."
- "About the only thing Paul and I had in common was a dislike for Earl Weaver. Earl has brought a lot of people together that way."

Bill James One-liners

Bill James is the author of the *Baseball Abstract* books and one of the best baseball analysts around. He's known mainly for his statistical analysis of the game, but he's not just a numbers man. He's got a wickedly sardonic sense of humor and a Henny Youngmanesque gift for the cutting one-liner. Herewith a few darts from the James quiver:

"Jim Frey's handling of his three catchers—Wathan, Grote and Quirk—ranks somewhere between 'maladroit' and 'lunatic.' "

"Like Ray Kroc, Ted Turner seems never to have been tempted by moderation, by dignity or restraint."

"The Polish Anti-Defamation League should protest Greg Luzinski's being required to play the outfield."

"[The 34-year-old Larry Bowa] has about as much range as the Birdman of Alcatraz."

"Ever notice how much Joe Torre looks like Rich Little? I keep expecting him to shake his jowls and do a little Tricky Dick for us."

"If Dallas Green thinks that lousy players are lousy players because they don't try hard enough, how does he explain his own career?" (After Green, as general manager of the Cubs, criticized his players for not trying hard enough.)

"The California Angels change their infield more often than their underwear."

"The Montreal Expos of Gary Carter's last years were a team with more holes than a porcupine's underwear." (Another variation on the underwear theme.)

"Terry Kennedy is slower than the fat girl chasing her chihuahua up the staircase."

"Trying to get rid of a losing attitude in Cleveland must be like trying to stamp out venereal disease around an Army base."

"If Henry Cotto is a major league ballplayer, I'm an airplane."

"Rick Cerone is to catching more or less what Thurman Munson was to aviation." (Ouch!)

Literary Criticism

Darryl, by Darryl Strawberry and Art Rust, Jr.

"Why would he bury his friend that way? It's weak and it's premeditated. This is a book, man. This isn't something he said off the top of his head after a game."
—Kevin Elster, after the book *Darryl*, speculated that Mets pitcher Dwight Gooden, a friend of Strawberry's, had used cocaine during the 1986 post-season

"I don't plan to read the book. I don't plan to read excerpts from the book. I don't want to know about the book."
—Frank Cashen, Mets executive

"It's garbage."
—Mets GM Al Harazin, whom Strawberry accused of favoring white players over black ones

"I could care less what the Mets think about me . . . Whoever don't like it, too bad."
—Touchy author Darryl Strawberry, responding to criticism of his work

Nails by Lenny Dykstra

"If you take out the fucks, this is an 18-page book."
—Wally Backman, thumbing through the autobiography of his Mets teammate

If At First . . . by Keith Hernandez

"If At First *is the diary of a human wart. Hernandez seems to think there is no clause in the human contract that holds one accountable for behaving like a pig."*
—John Gregory Dunne, novelist

Ball Four by Jim Bouton with Leonard Shecter

"Fuck you, Shakespeare!"
—Pete Rose, calling out to Bouton on the mound after the publication of the controversial, tell-all book

"Jim who?"
—Mickey Mantle, one of the unwitting stars of the book, when asked about it

"You've done the game a grave disservice. Saying players kissed on the team bus—incredible!"
—Bowie Kuhn, then baseball commissioner, in a note to Bouton

"I feel sorry for Jim Bouton. He is a social leper. He didn't catch it, he developed it. His collaborator on the book, Leonard Shecter, is a social leper. People like this, embittered people, sit down in their time of deepest rejection and write. They write, oh hell, everybody stinks, everybody but me, and it makes them feel much better."
—Dick Young, *Daily News* columnist

Insult Headlines

"THE BOYS OF SLAMMER."
—*New York Daily News*, after some Mets players were arrested in 1986 after a fight in a Houston bar

"WAIT TILL NEXT YEAR!"
—*Boston Herald*, after the Red Sox lost on Opening Day of the 1988 season

"WILSON: GOOSE IS A TURKEY!"
—*New York Post*, after Glenn Wilson allegedly criticized Yankee pitcher Goose Gossage (whenever Goose got shelled, New York newspapers would frequently compare him to Ben Franklin's favorite bird)

"YOUR WORST NIGHTMARE COMES TRUE: HE'S BAAAAACK!"
—*Boston Herald*, after former Red Sox manager Don Zimmer was rehired as a coach in 1991

"FROM DYNASTY TO DIE-NASTY."
—*San Francisco Chronicle*, after the "invincible" Oakland A's got swept by Cincinnati in the 1990 World Series

"JAYS END AN EMBARRASSING JOKE."
"JAYS MUST WAIT UNTIL NEXT YEAR—AGAIN!"
—Headlines in Toronto papers after the Blue Jays lost yet another LCS in 1991

Two Guys who See the Poetry in Baseball

Not everybody loves George Will. Can you believe it? He wrote a best-selling book, *Men at Work*, which characterizes A's manager Tony LaRussa as a strategic genius. After LaRussa froze up in Game 2 of the 1990 World Series, leaving the struggling Bob Welch in the game too long, Bill Conlin cracked, "If Will writes a sequel, perhaps he should call it *Men Asleep On The Job.*"

We also feel obliged to pass along Rick Reilly's comment about Will and filmmaker Ken Burns and their romantic view of baseball. Says Reilly:

"Ken Burns, the director of the brilliant PBS documentary "The Civil War," says he will spend the next four years of his life making a series on baseball. Nice. First George Will, now this guy. This kills me. Most baseball players barely get out of high school, won't read anything that doesn't have an ad for X-Ray Specs in the back and spend an inordinate percentage of their lives trying to see how many jockstraps they can fill with Nair. Yet up in the press box, guys like Burns and Will, guys who look like high-school equipment managers, are assembling 30-hour films and 200-page treatises on the historic importance of the infield fly rule."

. . . And One Guy Who Doesn't

"Baseball is a game that used to be played by Babe Ruth and Ty Cobb, and then by Joe DiMaggio and Ted Williams, and then by Mickey Mantle and Willie Mays. Now it's a game that's played by a bunch of guys in leotards and helmets on wall-to-wall carpet, with Tommy Lasorda discussing pasta and cavorting with movie stars."

Dan Jenkins may be the world's greatest sportswriter—then again, he may not be—but he has one serious flaw. He doesn't like baseball.

"Baseball mainly attracts two democratic groups: boys under 14 and men over 60. Boys under 14 like it because their daddies made them play catch in the yard. Men over 60 like it because they have to piss a lot and they can do this while watching baseball on TV and not miss anything."

Jenkins, whose favorite sports are golf and college football, says that baseball is boring. To remedy this problem he suggests going immediately from Opening Day to the playoffs and World Series. "What do we lose," as he says, "a few stats?"

Oh well. To each his own, and all that. And Jenkins does admit there are times when baseball gets his blood going: "Occasionally, baseball gets exciting for everybody. That's when the World Series reaches the ninth inning of the seventh game and the score is tied. For the next two and a half hours, even I am enthralled."

Press Paranoia: A Multiple Choice Quiz

Match the paranoid and/or hyper-defensive statement about the press with the ballplayer who said it. Answers are at bottom.

1) "The New York writers are paid to try to start feuds."
a) Graig Nettles b) Donald Trump c) Darryl Strawberry d) David Dinkins

2) "I'm not the crazy, out-of-control dirtbag that people think I am."
a) Mike Tyson b) Donald Trump c) Lenny Dykstra d) Rob Dibble

3) "The media around Cincinnati perceives me as an ax murderer. They don't give me any respect."
a) Lizzie Borden b) Rob Dibble c) Pete Rose d) Sam Wyche

4) "Oh I hated that Boston press. I can still remember the things they wrote, and they still make me mad."
a) Carleton Fisk b) Michael Dukakis c) Ted Williams d) The Boston Strangler

5) "I'm tired of seeing my picture on the front page of USA Today. That's the only paper I get. But you can't put much stock in papers. They only cost 50 cents."
a) Leona Helmsley b) Jose Canseco c) Pete Rose d) David Cone

6) "There are three thousand sportswriters, and they're all against me."
a) Bobby Knight b) Joaquin Andujar c) Jose Canseco 4) George Steinbrenner

7) "Do you know how many people want to read dirt about me? A lot. Obviously, I'm an important person. The media blow what I say out of proportion and make me look like an ass."
a) Bobby Bonds b) Barry Bonds c) James Bond d) Michael Milkin, king of the junk bonds

8) "I wouldn't want to be a writer. Some are probably jealous that this prima donna ballplayer making a lot of money won't help them write their little articles."
a) Darryl Strawberry b) Charles Barkley c) Rob Dibble d) Dave Kingman

9) "Somebody twisted my words. I'm not talking to reporters any-more. We Latins have to stick together."
a) Ricardo Montalban b) Julio Franco c) Roberto Alomar d) Charo

10) "How can they let a girl go on 'A Current Affair' and say she was my lover? They probably paid her for it. Anybody could go on TV and make any kind of accusation they wanted."
a) Geraldo Rivera b) Bill Clinton c) Jose Canseco 4) Steve Garvey

1 (a), 2 (c), 3 (b), 4 (c), 5 (c), 6 (b), 7 (b), 8 (d), 9 (b), 10 (c)

Going...
Going...
Gone!

S ome of these guys are dead and gone. Some of these guys are gone from baseball but not dead. Some of these guys appear to be dead but are still involved in the game; they're called coaches. One or two of these guys are active players but on their way out. Then there's a final group of guys who are retired from baseball and who should stay away permanently. We'll let you decide who fits into what category.

Billy

Billy Martin is definitely dead. But who can forget him? Not ex-Yankee GM Al Rosen, who disliked him intensely. "I couldn't warm up to him if I were embalmed with him," said Al.

Nor could Richie Phillips and the members of his umpires' union. "Billy Martin is going to have to sit in the dugout from now on with his hands folded and his lips closed like a choir boy," Phillips said after a 1988 incident in which Billy was suspended for kicking dirt on an umpire, a favorite pastime of his. "We will no longer tolerate his tap room behavior."

Billy had a thing against umps. "Seattle's best player out there today was the second base umpire," he said, feeling cheated after some calls went against the Yankees. Billy always suspected that people were trying to cheat him. "There's no question we were cheated," he said after American League commissioner Lee MacPhail ruled against New York in the celebrated pine tar bat brouhaha in 1983. In this case, at least, he had a point. He had caught George Brett dirty-handed, but

Billy Martin often felt that people were out to get him—and many times they were.

the men in the ties had taken it away from him. "They ought to call the rule book the funny pages. All it's good for is when you go deer hunting and run out of toilet paper," Billy said disgustedly.

Ed Figueroa will never forget Billy. And boy, was he glad when mellow Bob Lemon replaced Martin as manager of the Yankees in 1978. "Billy thinks he knows pitching. He doesn't know shit," said Figgy. "He hurts pitchers because he doesn't know how to use them. And he screws pitchers up because he always wants to call all the pitches." Other people said the same thing—that he hurt pitchers' arms—but Billy basically blew them off and you didn't argue with Billy unless you wanted to fight. ("Everybody looks up to Billy," goes the joke, "because he probably just knocked them down.")

Reggie Jackson, Billy's nemesis, will never forget those days. Nor will the third member of that unholy triad, George Steinbrenner. The Boss hired and fired Billy five times as manager of the Yankees and after the second time, a bitter Martin said, "George was born very rich and he thinks everyone can be bought and then he finds someone who can't be bought . . . I feel the man is sick, I'll be honest with you. I'll only go back if George is gone." But Billy came back of course, again and again.

Somewhere out there, there's a marshmallow salesman who can't forget him. Ed Whitson, who fought and whipped Billy, won't forget him. Jerry Coleman, who played with him on the Yankees, won't forget that look on Martin's face when somebody tried to push him around: "Like a small rodent that had been backed into a corner." Tom Boswell called him "a walking psychodrama." Lighter in tone, but along the same lines, was Mike Downey's observation of the Martin style of baseball management: "Billy Martin makes the game lean a little more toward professional wrestling. He might as well wear a hood and come to the park as the Masked Manager."

Yes, it was a freaking circus out there with Martin running the show. But damn, the man sure knew baseball, didn't he?

Some Thoughts From Billy About Reggie Jackson

"I'm sick and tired of this crap. We've got a smooth-running ship here, and I don't want him coming along and breaking it up. If you want to play ball, Reggie, fine—then shut your mouth and play."

—In 1977, after their famous nationally televised near-fight in the Yankee dugout

"Reggie Jackson could never be a true Yankee. Yankees care about other Yankees. Reggie just cared about Reggie."

"I never pay any attention to anything Reggie says anyway. Why should I? His teammates don't."

"Leadership is done by example, not by mouth."

Aw, Come on Billy, Off the Record, What'd You Really Think of Reggie?

"Off the record, he's a piece of shit."
—As quoted by baseball historian Bob Chieger

Now, Billy Talks About a Few of His Managerial Peers

"Let's just say that Williams certainly was one of the greatest hitters of all time. Also one of the lousiest managers of all time."
—On Ted Williams, former manager of the Senators

"To me, he's the classic case of the guy who overmanages. He tries to be so brilliant. He takes the game away from his players. His problem is that he often tries to show how much he knows, how much more he knows about the game than the guy in the other dugout, and it backfires on him. . . . I just let him make his moves and I just sit back and wait until he outsmarts himself."
—On Gene Mauch, the "Little General"

"What does Weaver know about throwing at guys? He never played in the big leagues. He must have read about it in The Lou Gehrig Story.*"*
—After Earl Weaver of the Orioles accused Martin's Yankees of throwing at his players in a 1978 game

Billy and Henry Hecht

Billy Martin didn't get along with Reggie Jackson, marshmallow salesmen, bartenders who said no, and Henry Hecht. Hecht was a sportswriter for the *New York Post* when Martin managed the Yankees in the seventies and eighties, and they basically hated each other's guts. Martin thought Hecht was a Steinbrenner spy, and Hecht thought Martin was a louse who couldn't manage his way out of a paper bag.

Graig Nettles didn't like Hecht either. In Nettles's book he called him "the worst" of the sportswriters who go out of their way to put the knock on ballplayers. "If you mess up a play," said the Yankee third baseman, "he'll gladly write how poor you're doing, but if you make a great play—or three great plays—there'll be no mention of it. He's like a vulture eager to pounce on an erring ballplayer." Hecht might say in response that ballplayers get paid a lot of money for what they do; they should be able to take the criticism.

Nettles was in the Yankee locker room for the 1983 team meeting when Billy Martin went into one of his greatest-ever snits, one that should be ranked alongside his famous "One's a born liar, the other's convicted" remark about Reggie Jackson and George Steinbrenner, his many duke-outs with players and fans, the notorious Copacabana bust-up with Mickey Mantle and Whitey Ford in the fifties, and the time he destroyed his office as manager of the Oakland A's. This time, the object of his rage was Hecht.

In an article in the *Post* earlier in the year Hecht had accused Martin of telling the Yankee players to ignore what George Steinbrenner said to them (sensible advice, I say!). But Martin said this was a lie and at a clubhouse meeting with other reporters and the Yankee team looking on, he singled Hecht out.

"You see this little scrounge right here?" he said, pointing to the diminutive Hecht. "This is the worst fucking scrounge to ever come around this clubhouse. He got me fired twice, and he's trying to get me fired again. Any of you guys talk to this little scrounge, don't talk to me, 'cause I don't want to have anything to do with anyone who talks to this little prick."

Hecht replied that Martin was "paranoid" and Billy really blew then. "I'm not paranoid. I don't have to be paranoid to see that you're a little prick. You're not welcome in my office. You can come into the clubhouse—I wouldn't ever take away a man's right to earn a living—but you're not welcome in my office because I don't trust a fuckin' thing you say. If you come in my office I'll dump you in the whirlpool. If you were a big enough man, I'd dump you right now. What do you think of that?"

"You can imagine what I think of you, Billy," said Hecht.

"Yeah, I know," said Martin. "I read the shit every day."

After Martin cooled down and the meeting broke up, Nettles,

who was one of Billy's favorite ballplayers, was giggling about it. "We finally had a clubhouse meeting that made sense," he said.

More Barbs and Nettles by Graig Nettles

"To do Tiant's, they'll have to get a harpoon."
—Upon learning that all Yankee players, including the pudgy Luis Tiant, would have to get inoculations for hepatitis

"What does he need another candy bar for? He's already got one—Butterfingers."
—After hearing that Reggie Jackson had just had a candy bar named after him

"Bowie finally made a correct decision. He finally made one good decision for the good of baseball. He resigned."
—On the resignation of Commissioner Bowie Kuhn (whom Nettles referred to as "Buffoon Bowie")

"I'd rather have my kids find a Hustler *magazine around the house than a* New York Post.*"*
—Registering his disgust for the New York tabloid

"He's the only guy in baseball who gets to wear his place of residence on his back."
—On tough-guy Cleveland outfielder Wayne Cage, who wore his last name on his uniform

"If you killed a few of the flies, it would be a big improvement."
—Asked by a Seattle locker room attendant how he rated the Mariners clubhouse

He May Never Make the Hall of Fame, But He Sure Had a Way with Words, Didn't He?

Before he came to the Yankees Goose Gossage pitched for the White Sox and the Pirates, and when he was with the Sox he faced Thurman Munson in a game. But the Goose was young and wild then and one of his 90-plus mph blue-plate specials got away from him and he plunked the Yankee catcher in the shoulder. Or maybe Gossage was aiming there; anyway, he gave Munson a good hard shot.

Munson only smiled, then jogged down to first without rubbing the spot or giving even the slightest indication that he felt any pain. He appeared to regard Gossage's heater no differently than if he had been grazed by butterfly wings.

Then, after the game was over, Munson sent a note over to Gossage in the White Sox clubhouse. "I took your best fucking shot, you cockroach," it said.

Bill Lee

Boston lefthander Bill Lee was more Spaceman than Insultman, but he had his moments. Such as his description of the New York Yankees in the era of the late seventies ("Billy Martin's brownshirts") or his praise for the federal judge who ordered school busing in racially divided Boston: "Judge Garrity's the only man in town with any guts." Lee was roundly criticized for this remark by Boston City Councilman Albert "Dapper" O'Neill, who wrote him a scathing letter that concluded that "on my worst day I could still outpitch you." Lee wrote back, "Dear Councillor O'Neill, I think you should be made aware that some idiot has gotten hold of your stationery . . ."

Some other Lee cracks from that time:

On the new orange roof at Montreal's Olympic Stadium: "It looks like the same thing George Scott wore around his waist when he was trying to lose weight."

On the bumbling good luck of Boston manager Darrell Johnson: "He keeps falling out of trees and landing on his feet."

On the coaching at his alma mater compared to Boston: "Rod Dedeaux teaches more in one season at USC than the Red Sox organization does in ten years."

On a weak-hitting team: "A bunch of hookers swinging their purses."

After a trip to China, he said this was a typical breakfast there: "Four-year-old eggs with green and blue yolks."

His reaction to what he saw as the hypocrisy of American League president Joe Cronin after Cronin fined Texas pitcher Jim Merritt for admitting he threw a spitter: "Tell Cronin I threw a spitter in Detroit a while back. Tiny Taylor hit it into the upper deck. Yes, I have a tube of K-Y jelly in my locker. So do a lot of other pitchers who throw it more often than I do. Hell, if K-Y jelly went off the market, the Angels whole staff would be out of baseball. So you'd better tell Cronin to fine me, too." (Cronin did.)

After his good friend Bernie Carbo was traded from the Red Sox to the Indians: "They keep saying we're all supposed to be a family here. If you're a family, you don't send your children to Cleveland."

And, after he nicknamed Don Zimmer "the designated gerbil," he said, "I guess I should have apologized—to the gerbils."

The Gerbil, aka Chiang Kai-Shek

Don Zimmer is and forever shall be the gerbil. Bill Lee designated him that and it's been his curse ever since. There's something about Zimmer's bulldog-with-elephantitis face that invites disdain. Or maybe it's the way he manages. Who can say for certain?

But Zim is a prideful man with a long background in baseball, and after the Cubs fired him early in the 1991 season he showed that he had a talent for sarcasm himself. "I want to know about the music," he told Bob Verdi later in the year. "When they got rid of me, that was the first thing [the players] complained about. I didn't let them blast the stereo in the clubhouse. I didn't mind the music. I just didn't like it when the walls shook. But hey, obviously I was wrong. After I left, I understand they went out and got new speakers so the music could be even louder. That made them all happy, and hey, it shows in the record. As soon as I got out of town, they started to win and they haven't stopped yet, right? I mean, they're going to be playing that music until they win the World Series, right?"

Zimmer went on, "What were they when they dumped me, a game under .500? And what are they now, one game under .500? I don't know about you, but that tells me they got things squared away up there."

Zimmer was sharply criticized in Chicago for not batting Ryne Sandberg third in the lineup. The manager said he agreed with the fans, but his star second baseman wouldn't do it and he had to cover up for him. "I knew Sandberg should have been hitting third the last four or five years, but the guy didn't want to. He wanted to hit second, so that's where he hit. Whenever I was asked about it, I had to cover it up."

In addition, Zimmer said he wanted Sandberg to run more. "I wanted him to steal bases, but he only wanted to steal when he felt comfortable. He only wanted to steal when the count was right." (Zim may be onto something here. One columnist described the bland Sandberg as having the personality of "a Chia pet.")

Zimmer also took off on Cub broadcasters Steve Stone and Harry Caray, who led the chorus demanding Zimmer's head in his final days. "I heard from friends what a job Harry and Steve did on me the two weeks before I was fired. All I can say is Steve Stone is the smartest baseball man I've ever heard. He's beautiful." And, signing off, Zimmer expressed his fondest wishes for his former team: "I could care less whether they win or lose."

Still, Cub fans were mostly happy to see him go, particularly those like Tony Kornheiser who believed that his mismanaging cost the team whatever chance they had to beat San Francisco in the 1989 National League playoffs. "Zimmy, Zimmy, Zimmy, where'd you learn how to manage, from a Sears and Roebuck catalogue?" Kornheiser asked. "Zimmy, if this is seat-of-the-pants managing, maybe you ought to wear a dress next season."

Surely the strangest twist in Zimmer's career occurred after the Cubs' firing when, in the age-old baseball tradition of recycling old coaching fodder, the Red Sox hired him as their third base coach. *The gerbil . . . in Boston . . . again?* Except for any Yankee fan, Zimmer was probably the most reviled man in New England before he left, in 1980, on a fast train just barely ahead of the tar-and-feathers brigade. He took over the Sox in mid-1976 and oversaw the wreckage of that disastrous, gloom-laden (for Boston fans) 1978 campaign. Second-guessed for the way he handled pitchers, ridiculed for the way he looked and spoke, accused of being on "angel dust" by one radio announcer, Zimmer should've worn a bullseye on his back. Nor did he help his cause any by saying that Dwight Evans, the longtime Red Sox rightfielder, had "all the balls of a female cow." Callers to WHDH's "Sports Huddle" talk show could not refer to Zimmer by name; if they did they were cut off immediately. They had to refer to him by a code name: "Chiang Kai-Shek."

Playing Chairman Mao to Zimmer's Chiang Kai-Shek was Bill Lee, whose iconoclasm won points with Boston fans but pissed off his manager no end. Lee blamed Zimmer for Boston's collapse in 1978, in part for yanking him out of the starting rotation during the stretch drive. "He lost the pennant," Lee said years later about Zimmer. "We should've been home free. A manager shouldn't bury veteran ball-players. He shouldn't have buried me."

After being beaned as a young ballplayer, doctors put a corrective plate in Zimmer's head. The Spaceman thought this was the reason they never got along: "Zimmer's beanings as a player caused a pyschopathic dislike for pitchers." Lee called him "an SOB" after his good friend, Bernie Carbo, was traded from the Sox. He mocked the Zimmer-imposed dress code by wearing bowling shirts and going on team charters in his bare feet. "There's no way I can communicate with that man," said Lee, and his manager might've said the same thing about him. Zimmer detested Lee, saying that he was one of three people (the other two were Mike Torrez and Derrel Thomas) he'd never allow in his home.

"A lot of people around here are sick and tired of Bill Lee," said Zimmer, who won the war by shipping the lefthander off to Montreal after that disastrous 1978 season. Getting rid of the popular Lee did not endear Zimmer with Boston's fans, however, and they finally won *their* feud with him by seeing him fired two years later.

Potshots From the Past

"Could be that he's a nice guy when you get to know him, but why bother?"
—Hall of Famer Dizzy Dean, on another Hall of Famer, Bill Terry

"They shot the wrong McKinley!"
—Ol' Diz again, after arguing in vain over a call with umpire Bill McKinley

"He eats gunpowder every morning and washes it down with blood."
—Umpire Arlie Latham, on the combative New York Giants manager John McGraw

"Five thousand dollars? Fuck you, you little son of a bitch! Who the hell do you think you are? If you were even half my size I'd punch the shit out of you."
—The reported words of Babe Ruth to Yankee manager Miller Huggins, after Huggins fined him $5,000 for misconduct

"If it was within my power, I would have inscribed on Chapman's tombstone these words: 'Here lies the victim of arrogance, viciousness and greed.'"
—Ty Cobb, in a note to Carl Mays, referring to the man Mays killed with a fastball to the head, Ray Chapman

"The only difference now is that he is a bad guy who is dead."
—Obituary, on the death of the misanthropic Ty Cobb in 1961

"A chunky, unshaven hobo who ran the bases like a berserk locomotive, slept in the raw, and swore at pitchers in his sleep."
—Lee Allen, on the Wild Hoss of the Osage, Pepper Martin

"DiMaggio could have done all his hitting in a chimney."
—Bugs Baer, after Joe popped up to the catcher four times in a World Series game

"The last time I saw a pair of legs like that there was a message attached to them."
—Ralph Kiner, on pigeon-legged Catfish Metkovich

"Ralph Kiner has so many other weaknesses that if you had eight Ralph Kiners on an American Association team, it would finish last."
—Branch Rickey, on why he wasn't giving the Pirates slugging star a raise

"To say that Horace can drink is like saying that Sinatra can sing."
—Leo Durocher, on the legendary imbibing abilities of Giants owner Horace Stoneham

"They voted Casey the greatest living manager. That's a lot of bull—a joke. The only thing a manager has to do is relate to the players. Who did Casey ever relate to? Nobody but himself."
—Jackie Robinson, on Casey Stengel

"You big clown, it's a good thing you're not in my league. I'd have your job in a minute."
—A young Billy Martin, taunting fellow second-sacker Jackie Robinson

"I never felt as bad when my father died as when I was released by the Cardinals. The Cards were all fine, except one. That was Eddie Stanky."
—Enos Slaughter, on Eddie "The Brat," his last manager with St. Louis

"Fred Haney didn't manage the club. He sat in one corner of the dugout, gulping down pills and saying to Crandall, "What should we do, Del?"

—Pitcher Joey Hay, on the Haney-managed 1959 Milwaukee Braves

"He's a goddamn nut. A guy like that would hit a woman."

—Dodgers coach Danny Ozark on Juan Marichal, after the Giants pitcher clubbed John Roseboro with a bat during an infamous 1965 game

"He's an old thirty."

—Reds president Bill DeWitt, on why he traded Frank Robinson to the Orioles in 1966 (Robinson won the Triple Crown that year and led Baltimore to a World Series title)

"One of the more selfish players I've ever encountered."

—Frank Robinson, on fellow Hall-of-Famer Joe Morgan late in his career

"He showed me nothing. He wouldn't win five games in the National League."

—Pete Rose, after facing Luis Tiant in the 1975 World Series

"Talking to Scott is like talking to a cement wall."

—Boston manager Dick Williams, on his brick-headed first baseman George Scott

"I don't want to win my 300th game while he's still here. He'd take credit for it."

—Jim Palmer, on his manager and frequent foe, Earl Weaver

Larry Bowa, to shortstop rival Davey Concepcion: "Is your first name Elmer?"

Concepcion: "No, why?"

Bowa: "Because every time I look in the box score, I see E-Concepcion."

"One guy is finished, and the other guy is nuts."

—Toronto manager Bobby Cox, on his two designated hitters, Wayne Nordhagen and Dave Revering

First sportswriter, after watching Doug DeCinces boot a ground ball: "That was a real tough one, it hit a pebble at the last minute." Second sportswriter: "Yeah, if you call your knee a pebble."

Dave Parker, Former Pirates Star, Looks Back with Fondness on What It Was Like to Play in Steel City

"Of all the places I played, Pittsburgh is the most racist."

"A terrible town. They resented me there for being an outspoken black with a million-dollar salary."

"I hope Cincinnati wipes the Pirates out. I hate Pittsburgh and the front office and what they're all about. What they tried to do to one of the best players who ever played for them [Parker himself] was just a sleazy act. It was an attempt at a modern day lynching. There's no reason for me to be anything but bitter about it."

—Before the 1990 NLCS between the Pirates and Cincinnati

Two Close Observers Tell What It Was Like to Be Around Jim Rice Towards the End of His Career

"A bloated Brando/Elvis who could do nothing but sit in a corner of the dugout or clubhouse and snarl."

—Dan Shaughnessy, Boston sportswriter

"Team unity never existed from what I saw around the Sox clubhouse. Much of this problem results from the many years of the Jim Rice reign of the clubhouse. Rice is an evil, envious, jealous person. You can see it in his eyes, all you have to do is walk past him, and you can tell he is thinking nasty thoughts, and if you look back when you pass him, you see him whispering things behind your back to one of his allies. Rice's locker mate in 1986 was Don Baylor, and it didn't take Baylor long to figure out what kind of guy Rice was, because by the end of the season, it was obvious the two didn't care for each other. Rice was so hateful of Baylor."

—Longtime Red Sox employee, as quoted by Dan Shaughnessy

Dave Ding Dong

Dick Schaap was wrong about one thing (actually he's probably been wrong about a lot of things, but this is the only one I can pin down concretely). In writing about gargantuan slugger and even bigger pain-in-the-rear Dave Kingman, he referred to him as someone about "whose personality we can say absolutely nothing." This is untrue. You can say a number of things about Kingman's personality, though admittedly none of them is any good.

In the history of the baseball insult, Kingman occupies a prominent place if for no other reason than his notorious gift of a live rat to sportswriter Susan Fornoff when he played for the A's in the mid-eighties. This was not a nice gift, the way you might give a person a puppy or a parakeet. This was an act of spite; Kingman, never a friend of the Fourth Estate, did not like Fornoff in the locker room—she is a woman *and* a sportswriter—and he sought to humiliate her. Fornoff's colleagues in the media then attacked Kingman, and in a show of support for their teammate whom they felt was being unfairly picked on, the rest of the A's stopped talking to the press. Bill James drew a circle around the putrefied mess quite nicely: "Kingman has always been dismissed as an immature jerk. It turns out that all he needed was the right team to bring out this new side of his personality, a team full of immature jerks. The A's were able to oblige."

Kingman hit over 400 home runs, enough to carry some other player—a player who could do something besides hit home runs and snarl, we should say—to the Hall of Fame. But the guy will never make it, and if he somehow does, Mike Royko has a suggestion. Playing for the Cubs one year, Kingman made a wild throw that rolled into the dugout at Wrigley, travelled through an open door and bounced into a bathroom toilet. "The immortal Dave 'Ding Dong' Kingman," cracked Royko. "If he's ever voted into the Hall of Fame, they should put the toilet bowl in there, too."

Remembering Alex

Remember Alex Johnson? Probably you don't, and it's just as well. He played for a handful of teams in the sixties and seventies and he was about as lovable a fella as Kingman. Alex was a guy who could really, really get sick about a thing. You don't believe me? Just listen to him: "Ever get sick of a thing? I mean sick, sick, sick? I mean really sick, sick, sick? That's the way it is with me and this club. I didn't consciously decide to do this. But things are just so disgusting, it drills on my mind, drills on my mind."

What drilled on Alex's mind so much was the fact that he played for the California Angels—a team, you may have noticed, that he was sick of. So Alex went on a hunger strike or some such thing, refusing to give his all for the club, and the Angels got a little sick of that themselves and suspended him for ten days.

Another thing that made Alex sick was the media. He seldom talked to them much to begin with, and he did not exactly resemble Dan Quisenberry when he did. Early in his career a reporter asked him what was the difference between his rookie season, when he hit four home runs, and his second year when he had eight, "Four, you mother-fucker, four!" said Alex.

Now We Know Why They Used to Call Steve Garvey "Iron Man"

Now let's get this straight. Steve was married to Cyndy and they divorced. While still married to Cyndy, Steve took up with Judith and moved in with her. While living with Judith he met a woman named Rebecka and then proposed to *her.* Shortly after learning that Rebecka was carrying his baby, Steve decided that maybe marriage wasn't such a good idea after all.

About this time Steve met a third woman (or fourth, counting Cyndy) named Cheri, who later had a daughter—*his* daughter. Then, while seeing both Cheri and Rebecka, Steve met Candace, who must have been really special because he decided to marry her. Not only that, he actually went through with it.

Now here's the really bizarre thing. Somewhere in the midst of all this frenetic activity, Steve took up with Margo Adams, Wade Boggs's former lover, and had an affair with *her* too.

Aw, Steve, You should've stuck to baseball. It's a lot simpler.

"The last time I was surrounded by this many beautiful women was when I spent Father's Day at Steve Garvey's house."
—Bob Hope, at the 1989 Oscar award ceremonies

"The Surgeon General is stepping up his campaign about condom use. In fact, last night he even mentioned Steve Garvey by name."
—Jay Leno

"HONK IF YOU'RE CARRYING STEVE GARVEY'S BABY!"
"STEVE GARVEY: FATHER OF OUR COUNTRY."
"STEVE GARVEY: HE'S NOT MY PADRE!"
—Bumperstickers that appeared after the Garvey scandal became public in 1989

Bad judgment and a raging case of hormones brought down Steve Garvey, here seen in a team shot from his "Mr. Clean" days with the Dodgers.

"The guy is a sociopath. He needs therapy. I know I've had a lot of therapy in my life because of Steve Garvey."
—Cyndy Garvey, Steve's first wife

"As far as a lover, he's much better than Wade."
—Margo Adams, comparing Garvey and Boggs in the sack (but it's really more of an insult to Boggs, isn't it? Or is it?)

The Only Joke We've Ever Seen Involving Steve Garvey, Wade Boggs, and Pete Rose

Garvey, Boggs and Rose are all sitting at a bar when a beautiful blonde walks in.

Boggs sees her first and says, "I slept with her."

"Yeah," says Garvey quickly, "but she's carrying my baby."

"Don't bet on it," says Rose.

The Whiner

Mike Marshall was supposed to be the second coming of Steve Garvey. Mike didn't make it, either in the baseball or the fatherhood sense. After leaving the Dodgers, Marshall went to the Mets in 1990, where he publicly pouted because he wasn't starting. "Is that what he said?" said one Mets player, after being told that Marshall had asked for a trade. "Fuck him. Get rid of him. We don't need him."

From New York, Mike journeyed up to Boston, where he made another lasting impression. "You know that skit 'Saturday Night Live' did a few years ago called 'The Whiners'?" said Allan Siegel, a Boston broadcaster. "That skit was about Mike Marshall. When he went on the DL, it was a classic case of addition by subtraction. The Red Sox should just admit their mistake and get rid of him." The Red Sox did indeed admit their mistake and got rid of Marshall so that he could search about for some other ballclub to complain about. Said Toronto GM Pat Gillick: "Marshall likes to complain about not playing, but that's what he does best: not play."

The Goat

Lonnie Smith survived drug problems and a Dr. Strangeglove fielding reputation ("He needs one of those coal miner's hats, and turn the light on," said one writer after watching him misjudge a fly ball) to carve out a pretty respectable career in baseball. But he will never live down his Game 7 baserunning flub that enabled the Twins to outlast the Braves in that memorable 1991 World Series. His failure to score on the double by Terry Pendleton ranks as one of the all-time boners in Series history.

Did Lonnie buy the deke put on by Minnesota second baseman Chuck Knoblauch, causing him to hesitate and slow down even as the Twins outfielders were running like wild men after Pendleton's ball? "That decoy story is a bunch of manure," said Braves manager Bobby Cox. "If Lonnie had been decoyed, he would have slid into second base instead of running 20 feet past the base and then just standing there." Smith himself has offered muddled testimony, although he finally admitted that yes, Knoblauch's Little League maneuver did fool him.

Immediately after the game, inside the despondent Atlanta locker room, Lonnie wasn't saying anything, though. "There was one man . . . who acted like a spoiled little kid—one man who lost any sense of professionalism," observed San Francisco sportswriter Bruce Jenkins, who was there. "It was the man with the most explaining to do, and he shirked all responsibility for it. That man was Lonnie Smith."

Other Braves stepped up to try to find words to describe their disappointment. Not Smith. "Smith, when it came down to interrogation time, showed no class at all," said Jenkins. "This longtime veteran, the ultimate 'guy who's been around,' acted like a punk from reform school."

Smith hid in the showers to avoid reporters' questions. When he finally emerged a reporter asked him the big question: Did he pick up Pendleton's ball off the bat?

Lonnie barked, "What the hell game were you watching?"

"The same one you were," said the reporter.

"Evidently you weren't. It was such a stupid question," said Smith, and walked away.

You gotta feel a little bit sorry for Lonnie. Here he was, moments after falling for The Deke That Will Live Forever, probably feeling as if he cost his club the World Series, and he has to deal with a mob of reporters wanting to shine the lights on him and interrogate him. Still, that's baseball. And he'd better get used to questions about that play. Because they're going to follow him wherever he goes, as long as he lives. Just ask Bill Buckner.

Poor Billy B

Poor Billy Buckner. So miserable is his fate that he could almost be a figure in a child's nursery rhyme:

> Poor Billy B
> The ball rolled through his legs.
> He'll never live it down, you see,
> Poor Billy B.

Buckner, of course, made a crucial error in Game 6 of the 1986 World Series that cost Boston the game and a chance to win its first title in eons. Few people remember the wild pitch that Bob Stanley made that let in the tying run in that game. What they remember is Buckner's folly, and years later, when another Red Sox baseman, Carlos Quintana, lets a ball roll through his legs and a teammate yells out, "Nice play, Buckner!" we all know what he's referring to.

Question: What do Michael Jackson and Bill Buckner have in common?

Answer: They both wear a glove on one hand for no apparent reason.

Variations of that joke have been told about other players besides Buckner, but only this gag could apply to Poor Billy B. Utterly and totally depressed after making the error in Game 6, Buckner decided to end it all. So he walked out of the clubhouse and jumped in front of a car coming down the street. But the car went through his legs. . . .

Leo the Lip

Leo Durocher was the Billy Martin of his time: feisty, irascible and widely despised. "He is the king of the complainers, the trouble-makers, the malcontents," said ump Jocko Conlan, "the ones who can never, never, never accept a tough decision against them." Sounds a bit like Billy, doesn't it?

Ron Luciano said that Durocher was the kind of person who, if he patted you on the back, you halfway expected him to be holding a knife when he did it. He was a schemer and a conniver who wouldn't help an old lady across the street if he didn't see something in it for him on the other side. "You and Durocher are on a raft," goes Dick

Young's famous description. "A wave comes and knocks him into the ocean. You dive in and save his life. A shark comes and takes your leg. Next day, you and Leo start even."

Durocher died at 86 in 1991 in Palm Springs, a figure from another era. He played on the Gashouse Gang and managed the New York Giants when they fired the Shot Heard 'Round the World. More ignominiously, he was suspended in 1947 for a year for associating with gamblers—"a discredit to baseball," Commissioner Happy Chandler called him—and he presided over the Cubs' collapse in 1969, one of the saddest of all seasons in that club's history.

He gained immortality through one indelible utterance ("It's not whether you win or lose, it's how you play the game"—uh no, that was somebody else), and he became known as "The Lip" because he was never shy about expressing his opinions, even if they were of the negative variety. One time the president of NBC-TV asked him over to his table at a restaurant in New York City where they were both eating. The Lip declined the offer, saying: "I don't table hop, I don't eat with drunken bums, and as far as I'm concerned, you should be eating out of a trough." And Durocher was working for NBC as a baseball analyst at the time.

Like Tartuffe, many people did not appreciate Leo's form of candor, particularly the umpires for whom he reserved the bulk of his vitriol. "Call me anything," said ump Harry Wendelstedt, "call me motherfucker, but don't call me 'Durocher.' A Durocher is the lowest form of living matter." Babe Pinelli may have been the most amiable umpire of all time, but Leo could drive even him to thoughts of violent revenge. One time Durocher and Brooklyn's Carl Furillo got into a fight, with Carl on top choking Leo on the ground. Duke Snider, who was trying to separate the two, looked over and saw Babe Pinelli standing by: "Leo is turning white, I'm afraid he's going to die, and there's Babe Pinelli, Mr. Nice Guy—in all his umpire's neutrality—yelling, 'Kill him, Carl. Kill him!' "

But let's not leave this little remembrance on such a bloodthirsty note. There are many other funny Durocher stories. Joe Garagiola tells one about playing for the Durocher-managed Giants and striking out his first time up. His second time up, Joe hits a line drive back to the pitcher who doubles the runner off at first. "Next time," says Leo when Garagiola gets back to the bench, "why don't you just strike out and keep the inning going?"

Or, there was the big league outfielder who asked Durocher what he thought about him becoming a pitcher. "You could probably be a pitcher," replied Leo. "You hit like one." But my favorite Leo insult came when he was managing the Cubs and the weak-hitting Paul Popovich stood up to go into the game. "Sit down, Paul," said the Lip. "We ain't giving up yet."

Casey's Mets

More than three decades after they played, Casey's Mets are still entertaining us. One of the worst ballteams ever, they remain one of the most beloved. This is due, in large part, to the genius that was Casey Stengel, who had the unique gift of being able to insult people without offending them.

On Jay Hook, his Northwestern-educated pitcher, Casey said, "I got the smartest pitcher in the world until he goes to the mound." Another college-educated pitcher on those 1962 Mets was Craig Anderson, who was investing some of his salary in stocks. "He's got annuities," said his manager, "but he won't knock a batter on his butt."

One time Casey piled into a cab with a few of the writers who were covering the team. "Are you fellows players?" the cabbie asked. "No, and neither are my players," said Casey. Asked if he thought a planned exhibition tour in the high altitude climes of Mexico City would hurt his club, Casey replied, "No. We can lose at any altitude."

That first spring, after the expansion New York Metropolitans were formed, no one could have known how bad they'd be. But Casey knew. After the Mets upset the powerful Yankees in a spring training game, Casey said, "We wouldn't have done so good if their team was trying." Given the key to New York City prior to the start of the season, Casey said, "I got a lot of keys to a lot of cities, but this one I'm gonna use to open a new team."

Some of those old Mets are as well known as Hall of Famers. The immortal Choo Choo Coleman was a catcher who was good at handling low-ball pitchers because, as Casey said, "he crawls on his belly like a snake." Choo Choo was extremely fidgety behind the plate, so much so that when a Mets pitcher was asked to name the toughest man in the league to pitch to, he said Coleman.

Don Zimmer started the 1962 season as a Mets infielder. He started out hitting 3 for 12 before falling into a 0 for 34 slump. He broke out of the slump with a double and was traded two days later. "They traded him while he was hot," said one reporter.

And who can forget Marvelous Marv Throneberry, who achieved cultural hero status in New York while playing first base like a clown. After the 1962 season, in which he contributed mightily to the team's 120 losses, Throneberry had the effrontery to ask Johnny Murphy, who handled salary negotiations, for a raise.

"People came to the park to holler at me, just like Mantle and Maris," Throneberry said. "I drew people to the games."

"Yeah," said Murphy, "but you drove some away, too."

"I took a lot of abuse," Throneberry countered.

"And you brought most of it on yourself," said Murphy.

"But look," said Throneberry, growing desperate, "I played in the most games of my career: one hundred sixteen."

"But you didn't play well in any of them," replied Murphy calmly.

Ah, but none of those Mets played well, and that was the beauty of it. Leave it to their manager to sum it up: "The public that has survived one full season of this team has got to be congratulated."

Umps and Other Marginalia

This is the chapter with all the leftover insults that wouldn't quite fit anywhere else, with a special nod to those hardworking, under-appreciated men in blue.

Ump Insults

A book of baseball insults wouldn't be complete without a chapter on umpire insults, even though they tend to be the lamest jokes in baseball. Consider the story of how umpire Augie Donatelli was running his fingers through Don Drysdale's hair checking for possible illegal substances that he was using to load up the ball. Finding none, Augie turned to go back to home plate.

"Aren't you forgetting something, Augie?" Drysdale asked.

"What's that?"

"Well," he said, "usually when somebody runs their fingers through my hair, they also give me a kiss."

The Dodger righthander was spared ejection, which was not the case with California Angels manager Doug Rader after what he was certain was a foul ball was called fair, resulting in a home run for the Frank Robinson–managed Orioles and a loss for his club. Replays showed the ball hit the foul pole at Baltimore's old Memorial Stadium, and Rader was livid about this: "What a joke. It's enough to make you puke. 47,000 people left here knowing the ball was foul and they're going to try to sell that bill of goods? Give me a bucket. But it figures, come this close to Washington D.C. where they try to sell that stuff all the time."

*No, these umpires are not doing aerobics; they're practicing their "Safe!"
calls at an umpire school in Florida, showing why they're the butt of
so many baseball jokes.*

The next day, a still-seething Rader met the umpires at home plate for the customary pre-game conference. "Wait a minute," he said, glancing at Baltimore's score card. "There are four names missing from their lineup."

"Whose?" said the umps.

"Yours," said Rader.

But this was not sufficient to get him ejected. That occurred when ump Ken Kaiser showed up at the conference a few minutes late. "A little late coming out today, eh Ken?" said Rader. "Where were you, back in the Orioles locker room sitting on Frank Robinson's lap?" And he was gone.

More Ump Insults

"The FAA now says that if you're visually impaired or obese, you cannot sit next to any of the exits on an airplane. So if you're a major league umpire, you're just going to have to sit somewhere else."
—Jay Leno

"One day someone told me that my girlfriend would be arriving at the park in the fifth inning. I'm thinking: What girlfriend? I don't have a girlfriend . . . Then, in the fifth inning, the Goodyear Blimp flew over-head."
—Umpire Eric Gregg, who once weighed close to 400 pounds, telling the joke on himself

Dizzy Dean, in an argument with umpire George Barr during the 1934 World Series, demanded an answer from Barr about a call he made.

"I answered your question," said Barr. "I shook my head."

"No you didn't," said Dean, " 'cause if you did, I would've heard it rattle."

Umpire to an arguing player: "I've had it. You better shut up or I'll bite your head off."

Player: "If you do, you'll have more brains in your belly than you've got in your head."

"Tell me, ump. How can you sleep with the lights on?"
—Amos Otis, questioning a call during a night game.

Insults About Umpires' Eyesight

Tommy Lasorda got into an argument with ump Eric Gregg, who didn't much like the fact that the Dodger manager was protesting his calls. "I'm out here busting my hump," said Gregg. "I'm giving you my best effort."

"I'm not questioning your effort," said Lasorda, "I'm questioning your eyesight."

A close call in a tight game went against them, and a bunch of Montreal Expo players rushed out of the dugout to confront the umpire. Leading the charge was manager Gene Mauch, who yelled, "The first guy who lays a finger on this blind old man is fined 50 bucks!"

Once there was this umpire who was being heckled from the stands by a particularly belligerent fan. The ump was getting upset until he realized that the fan was drunk, and so he tried to calm him down.

"That's all right," said the fan. "I told you you were blind and you told me I was drunk—but tomorrow I'll be sober and you'll still be blind."

Joe Sparks, Iowa City minor league manager, asked ump Joe West where the umpires were staying in town.

"The Holiday Inn," said West.

"That figures," said Sparks. "That's the only place in town with braille numbers in the elevator."

Earl Weaver, in a spat with an umpire, said that he knew the rules as well as the ump did. "And I've got a rulebook in the clubhouse to prove it," he said.

"Well," the ump responded, "I've got the book right here and I'll show you."

"That won't work," said Weaver, refusing to look at the book. "I can't read Braille."

After being called out on strikes during a 1991 game, Andre Dawson of the Cubs was so furious that he threw a bunch of bats onto the field from the dugout. For this act of insubordination he was fined and suspended for one game. Mailing in his $1,000 payment for the fine, he wrote on the check, "Donation for the Blind."

Clever Ump Replies to Insults About Their Eyesight, Brains, Manhood, Etc.

After Bill McGowan called a batter out on strikes, the man flew into a tantrum, unable to believe that the umpire had made the call he did. McGowan stayed cool in the face of the batter's protest.

"If you still think you're not out, look in the paper tomorrow morning," he said.

Another old-time ump, Bill Klem, called a strike on a batter, who stepped back out of the box and said that Klem had missed the pitch.

"Well, if I'd had a bat on my shoulder I wouldn't have," said Klem.

Reporter: "Why did you throw Pie Traynor out of the game?"

Klem: "He wasn't feeling well."

Reporter: "He looked all right to me."

Klem (shaking his head): "Well, that's what he told me. He said he was sick of my stupid decisions."

After Kirby Puckett of the Twins took a strike three call, he complained to ump Ken Kaiser, who bellowed: "You swing at a fucking ball in the dirt, you swing at a fucking ball over your head, and then you take one right down the middle of the plate. Go fucking sit down!" (Okay, so maybe it's not so clever, but at least it's to the point. . . .)

Bill Madlock, questioning Bruce Froemming on a call: "Where was the ball?"

Froemming: "What is this, a fuckin' quiz? Get outta here!"

"You stink!" the manager yelled after the home plate ump called one of his runners out on a close play at the plate. "Let me say it again. You stink!"

This, of course, was unacceptable to the man in blue, who gave the manager the thumb. As the manager was going back to the dugout to leave the game, the ump yelled, "Now, how do I smell from there?"

Sphincter Stories

All right, so this isn't *Madame Bovary* or *War and Peace*. This is a book of baseball insults, and as such it has a section in it entitled "Sphincter

Stories." Not "Sphinx Stories" or "Leonard Spinks Stories," but "Sphincter Stories." There's a difference, you know.

Actually, I was going to call this "Asshole Stories," but I thought there might be some dads and moms out there perusing their local bookstore looking for a gift for the 11-year-old Little Leaguer in their family. And I thought if they started flipping through the pages and came across "Asshole Stories," they might say, "Hmmn. Well, maybe not."

So I started thinking about this possibility and opted instead for "Sphincter Stories" because I thought a title like that might fool Mom and Dad. They might see the word "sphincter" and think it's some kind of new baseball pitch, sort of like the split-finger or forkball.

"Come on, Sonny. Throw that little sphincter over the plate. He won't hit it . . ." Anyway, that's how the title came into being. Now what's this section about?

Well, in baseball there are a number of great stories that depend on the word "asshole" (or some variation thereof) for their humor. A classic involves the Japanese ballplayer, Masahito Watanabe, who was playing in the minor leagues as part of a cultural exchange program with the United States. Masahito spoke no English except what he picked up and what other ballplayers taught him. So one day he was standing around and an umpire came up to him and asked how he was doing. "Kiss my black ass," said Masahito with a big grin.

Another asshole story has Jerry Reuss, the former Dodger pitcher, standing around the outfield shagging balls. He picks one up and tosses it into the infield where it hits the rookie Adam Peterson in the leg.

"You asshole," Peterson yells.

"What'd you call me?" said Reuss, not sure if he heard right.

"An asshole."

"Listen, buddy," says Reuss, who's now really steamed, "I've got more years in the bigs than you've been alive. How about showing some respect?"

"All right," says Peterson. "*Mister* Asshole."

Then there's my favorite: a classic ump-manager tale whose characters vary depending on which version you hear. The way I heard it, it was an argument between Lou Piniella, then managing the Yankees, and umpire Marty Springstead. Upset at how Springstead was calling the balls and strikes, Piniella came running out of the dugout to protest.

"Where the fuck was that pitch at?"

"Don't you know you're not supposed to end a sentence with a preposition?" said Springstead, thinking he was being clever.

"Okay," said Piniella. "Where the fuck was that pitch at, you asshole?"

Insults From the Movie *Bull Durham* (Written and Directed by Ron Shelton)

"All right, honey. Let's get down to it. How was Ebby Calvin La-Loosh?"
Well, he fucks like he pitches. Sort of all over the place."

"He's got a million-dollar arm, but a five-cent head." (On Ebby Calvin LaLoosh)

"I'm Crash."
"Annie Savoy. Wanna dance?"
"I don't dance."
"How embarrassing."

"From what I hear, you couldn't hit water if you fell out of a boat." (Old line, actually.)

"Good punch."
"I'm Crash Davis. I'm your new catcher and you just got lesson one. Don't think. It can only hurt the ballclub."

"You boys stopped fightin'? Pals now? That's good. I love a little macho male bonding. I think it's sweet, I do. Even if it probably is latent homosexuality being rechanneled."

"So is somebody going to bed with somebody?"
"Honey, you are a regular nuclear meltdown. You better cool off."

"I believe . . . the novels of Susan Sontag are self-indulgent, overrated crap."

"Your shower shoes have fungus on 'em. You'll never make it to the bigs with fungus on your shower shoes. Think class, and you'll be classy. If you win 20 in the Show you can let the fungus grow back on your shower shoes and the press'll think you're colorful. Until you win 20 in the Show, however, it means you're a slob."

"I know women like you. Ooh, I know women like you. You're a regular patron saint. Stray cats, lost causes or 6-foot-3 homeless studs."

"You guys. You lollygag around the infield. You lollygag your way down to first. You lollygag in and out of the dugout. Do you know what that makes you, Larry?"
"Lollygaggers."
"Lollygaggers!"

"You've got a Hall of Fame arm, but you're pissing it away."
"I ain't pissing nothin' away. I got a Porsche already. I got a 911 with a quadruphonic Blaupunkt."
"Christ, you don't need a quadruphonic Blaupunkt. What you need is a curveball."

"Having a conversation with you is like a Martian talking to a fungo."
"Oh cute. Real cute. You know, just because you manage to be clever sometimes and you have a nice smile does not mean you're not full of shit."

"Hey, he's just your old man. He's as full of shit as anybody."

Insult Nicknames

Carl Nichols, Houston's backup catcher, was known as "Warren Moon" because he played only once a week . . . When Jack Clark was going bad in Boston, fans started calling him "Jack the Rip-Off." But when Clark's bat came back the name-calling ceased . . . Mickey Rivers used to be called "The Chancellor" because, as his Yankee teammate Graig Nettles said, "He's least likely to be chancellor of anything. . . ." His teammates on the Reds called Norm Charlton "The Genius" because of his three majors at Rice University. Which is no insult except as, Vin Scully points out, "You can get the tag of 'genius' in major league baseball by carrying a hardback book."

Fergie Jenkins suggested that Don Zimmer's nickname should be "the Buffalo" rather than the Gerbil. Why Buffalo? "A buffalo is the dumbest animal on earth," said Fergie . . . Speaking of large animals, there was Hippo Vaughan, who, compared to football's Refrigerator Perry, was "a walk-in meat locker." So said one of his teammates anyway . . . On the opposite side of the spectrum we have Starvin' Marvin Freeman. Starvin' Marvin stood 6-foot-7 and tipped the scales at 180 pounds. Another nickname for him: Manute Basebol.

There's a growing number of people who want to see the Indians and Braves change their team nicknames, saying they're insulting to Native Americans. Mark Whicker has a word of advice for Ted Turner: "Whatever happens, let's hope Braves owner Ted Turner doesn't react spitefully and re-nickname his team in the image of the stupidest, clumsiest, laziest mammals in this nation. Call them anything, Ted. Except Senators."

Twins manager Tom Kelly was making a beeline for the men's room at the Salt Lake City airport when a couple of fans asked him for his autograph. "Right now, I'm going to urinate," Kelly told the fans, and the comment made it into the Minneapolis newspapers. Since then he's been referred to as Tom "I'm Going to Urinate" Kelly by some.

In 1990, when the Twins were going badly, they called Minnesota GM Andy MacPhail by another name, too—Andy MacFail . . . They dubbed Manager Rene Lachemann "Captain Nemo" for steering the Brewers down to the deepest depths of the AL East in 1984. It was also Lachemann who called former Mariner Steve Stroughter "Stevie Wonder." Explained Lachemann: "Every time they hit the ball to him you wonder what's going to happen."

And finally, in the locker room celebration following the O's 1969 pennant, Frank Robinson yelled, "Bring on Rod Gaspar!" Gaspar played for the National League–winning Mets, but Frank didn't quite have his name right, so a teammate corrected him: "Not Ron, *Rod*, stupid." So Robinson said, "All right then, bring on Rod Stupid!" Henceforth Gaspar's ballyard moniker would be Rod Stupid.

Four Slogans Spotted on the T-shirts of Red Sox Fans After Boston Lost That 1978 Playoff Game to the Yankees and Blew the Division Title

"Boston Is Dead"
"Red Socks Choke"
"Yaz Has VD"
"Boston Sucks"

Fans—Don't You Just Love 'Em?

The Bleacher Creatures of Tiger Stadium used to do my all-time favorite ballpark cheer. In a spinoff on the Miller Lite "Tastes great—Less filling" commercials, fans in one section of the bleachers would yell, "Eat shit!," while the opposite section would answer, "Fuck you!"

Then there was that Fenway Park craze a couple of years ago— "perverts on parade," one columnist called it—that permanently destroyed Boston's reputation as the home of more intellectual baseball fans. Guys in the bleachers would pass around a blowup doll of an anatomically correct woman and do lewd and suggestive things with it. Fenway officials quickly put a stop to the practice, and not a moment too soon I say. As one female Red Sox fan said, "You come here to watch the game. You don't really need to see men sucking on women's parts, even if they're plastic."

Smart-asses

After Pete Rose said, "Election to the Hall of Fame is the ultimate honor a baseball player can receive. I am hopeful that I will someday be in a position to be considered," Tom Boswell said, "Don't bet on it."

After Dave Parker, age 40 and nearing the end of a great career, said, "I'll know when I'm through as a player. All the great ones know before anyone else can tell them," Moss Klein wrote, "Based on his inability to handle a good fastball this season, Parker should prepare to have a conversation with himself."

After White Sox manager Jim Lefebvre explained that "the 'b' is silent" when pronouncing his name, Bernie Lincicome said, "Like George Bell with runners on base."

After Tommy Lasorda asked Jay Johnstone if he someday wanted to become a baseball manager, Johnstone replied, 'What, and end up looking like you?"

After a young Dodger recruit just up from the farm club asked where the whirlpool was, Tommy Lasorda replied, "Just stick your foot in the toilet and flush it."

After ump Al Clark ruled that Roger Clemens, normally an expert control pitcher, did not intentionally hit a Tiger batter after giving up back-to-back home runs to Detroit, Dan Shaughnessy said, "Sure, Al.

And John Sununu needs taxpayer limos to keep the country safe when he's going to stamp shows."

After Vada Pinson gave a tip on how to play center to the less than graceful Howard Johnson, Tom Boswell wondered if the tip was: "Wear a crash helmet."

Some years ago, after hearing that Gloria Wagner, wife of Cincinnati GM Dick Wagner, broke her wrist in a fall, Davey Concepcion said, "She really broke her wrist trying to get Wagner's wallet out of his hip pocket."

During a horrible season in San Francisco, after Giants coach Rocky Bridges noticed a sign at Candlestick Park that read "Real Grass, Real Sunshine, Real Ball," he remarked, "Well, two out of three ain't bad."

The Curious Case of the Man Who Insulted Himself Who Was Not Himself

Junior Ortiz, a reserve catcher for the Minnesota Twins, is known as a funny guy. But he wasn't having an amusing time of it late in the 1991 season. Batting on the Interstate—somewhere in the .100s—he thought he needed a change. So he cut off his beard and said that from now on he wanted to be known as Joe Ortiz.

"Junior has gone back to Puerto Rico," said Joe. "Joe is an entirely separate person. Joe is a nice guy."

Then Joe Ortiz played a game, went hitless in five trips, and decided to revert back to Junior.

"Joe stinks," explained Junior. "Junior is a jerk, but at least he could play. In this game, you have to be a jerk."

What Are George Bush and Dan Quayle Doing in a Book of Baseball Insults?

A cynic might reply: "What are George Bush and Dan Quayle doing *anywhere?* But that's really a topic for another day. . . .

The correct answer is that we found a baseball-related insult about Bush, who played first base for Yale in his college days, and his vice president, who was once told that he was going to throw out the first ball at a Baltimore Orioles game. "Why," said Quayle, "what's wrong with it?" This was actually the creation of the friendly folks at *Inside Sports* magazine. The next one is the responsibility of Jim Hightower, former Texas state agriculture commissioner, who used his knowledge of the game to deliver a cutting little jab at our 40th President's upper class origins:

"George Bush was born on third base and thinks he hit a triple," said Hightower.

Two Little Known Pitching Rotations

"Three men and a maybe."
—A Toronto sportswriter, describing the Jays starting rotation in 1991.

"Ferguson Jenkins, Steve Trout and figure it out."
—Robert Markus, on a Cubs pitching rotation of a few years back.

. . . And One Hitting the Cutoff Man Line

"When he punched Keith Hernandez in spring training last season, it was the only time that Darryl Strawberry hit the cutoff man all year."
—Sportswriter Steve Wulf, on the 1989 Hernandez-Strawberry scuffle when they both played for the Mets

Fashion Victims

"[They need] a fashion consultant for Scott Erickson. Talk about winning ugly. The guy looks like he's pitching in dress shoes and Gold Toe socks. Ugh."
—*Baseball America,* on the black shoe look of the Twins pitcher

"We're playing like a circus so we might as well dress like it."
—Phillies manager Nick Leyva, after his team wore special green St. Patrick's Day uniforms

"A kid in need of a haircut whose sport coat barely covered his wrists."
—Dan Daniel, on a young Mickey Mantle

"He looks like a pilgrim going out to shoot a wild turkey."
—Dave Hamilton, assessing teammate Clay Carroll's old-style shorts uniform that the White Sox wore in the late 1970s; (John Mayberry said the Sox looked so cute in their little outfits that he might kiss one of them when they reached first base).

"I'm going to retire. No way I wear those damn hotpants."
—Bobby Bonds, after being traded to those same White Sox

"The players today wouldn't be caught dead in baggy flannels; now it's skintight double knits, and designer hitting shirts. How can teams wear different colored shirts and pants? That's not the Pittsburgh Pirates, that's a softball uniform."
—Billy Crystal, comedian

"We've got to change these things. We need to start looking like a ballclub instead of like jailbirds. We look like Taco Bell."
—Garry Templeton, on the brown and orange Padres uniforms; (they've since been changed).

"Most sportswriters dress as if they just came back from watching the Grateful Dead in the rain."
—Jay Johnstone, on the ultimate fashion victims, the men who cover major league baseball games for a living

Hair

"It's like he went in and asked for a butch. The barber started from the bottom up. Then he got a phone call and had to leave."
—Manager Nick Leyva, describing Lenny Dykstra's shaved-on-the-sides, curly-on-top haircut

"Some people have noticed that Dave Winfield's hair is many shades darker since he joined the Angels. Not all of it stems from getting away from Steinbrenner. Some of it came from a bottle."
—Columnist Marty Noble, after Winfield went from New York to California

"Jack spent 20 minutes combing his hair and forgot to bring it."
—Comedian Royce Elliott, during a roast for Cubs broadcaster Jack Brickhouse

The Ultimate Unanswered Question About Baseball As Posed by a Television Talk Show Host

"Why do ballplayers have to scratch and spit so much?"
—Kathie Lee Gifford

Index

Photo Credits

A Word From the Author

Heard any good insults lately? If you have, drop a line to Kevin Nelson, P.O. Box 1221, Benicia, California 94510. Who knows? There could be a *Baseball's Greatest Insults Part III,* and if anybody wants to pass along some of the good put-downs they've heard or read, it would be much appreciated.

About the Author

Kevin Nelson is the undisputed leading authority on sports insults. He is the author of books on baseball and football insults, as well as three other books on sports. His next book will be *Basketball's Greatest Insults*.